DUCATI
SUPER SPORT

DUCATI
SUPER SPORT

Ian Falloon

Foreword by Ing. Massimo Bordi

Haynes Publishing

First published in November 1998

British Library Cataloguing in Publication Data:
A catalogue record for this book is
available from the British Library

ISBN 1 85960 412 9

Library of Congress catalog card no. 98-72318

Published by Haynes Publishing, Sparkford,
Nr Yeovil, Somerset, BA22 7JJ, UK.

Tel: 01963 440635 Fax: 01963 440001
Int. tel: +44 1963 440635
Int fax: +44 1963 440001

E-mail: sales@haynes-manuals.co.uk
Web site: http://www.haynes.com

Haynes North America, Inc.
861 Lawrence Drive, Newbury Park,
California 91320 USA

Designed & typeset by
G&M, Raunds, Northamptonshire
Printed and bound in Great Britain by
J.H. Haynes & Co Ltd, Sparkford

Contents

Foreword

by Ing. Massimo Bordi

In observing the evolution of Ducati motorcycles through time, we can identify fundamental steps that help us understand what Ducati is today.

The history of the engines has signified a

Though more involved with the desmoquattro, *Ing. Massimo Bordi, current manager of Ducati Motor SpA, has been associated with the Super Sport since he joined the company in 1978.*

reassertion of technological leadership. From the single-cylinder desmo 100cc–450cc of the 1950s until the 1970s, to the twin-cylinder bevel-gear engines of the 1970s and 1980s. Then from the twin-cylinder 500 with the belt camshaft drive of 1978 to the *desmoquattro* of 1986. The same engine that has been victorious many times on the racetrack.

Alongside the 'history of the engines', there is the story of the models that have left, and will leave, their mark in the world of motorcycles. The *Marianna*, Mk III 250, 750 Super Sport, Pantah, 851 and 916.

The 'Supersport' has been the longest lived and one of the most important. Born in 1970, the first versions with the bevel-gear 750 and 900 engines were made popular on the track with riders like Smart and Hailwood. The bike also marked the success of many other champions worldwide. The later version, with a 500cc to 750cc belt-drive engine, gained further recognition on the road and on the track. Since the early 1990s the 900 SS has significantly increased its sales volumes.

The newly styled Supersport is now launched with many improvements to the engine and cycle parts. This version is not designed for the track, but will continue to give enormous satisfaction to *Ducatisti* on the road. Light weight, simplicity and better handling will make this an inimitable and unique Ducati.

But history is still in the making …

Introduction and acknowledgements

No other model evokes the sporting spirit of Ducati more than the Super Sport. While the first Super Sport was a true race replica, the ethos of the model has changed in recent times, coinciding with the movement from Super Sport to Supersport. In the days when racing bikes were minimalist in their approach, the Super Sport was a direct descendent. Nowadays Ducati's racing programme has by necessity moved into the world of maximum technology, leaving the current Supersport as a continuation along the path created by the first Imola replicas of 1974, but no longer a race replica. All the ingredients of 1974 have, however, been maintained: maximum on-the-road performance achieved through a better balance of handling, horsepower and weight – SSs may have never been the fastest machines available, but they have always offered the rider the best possible enjoyment – and engines that produce usable mid-range power at the expense of the top-end, all in a narrow and compact package. Simplicity has been an important feature and Super Sports were created to appeal to those not requiring multi-valve cylinder heads, water-cooling, and rising rate suspension systems. They are motorcycles that communicate directly with the rider without intimidation.

Right from its inception the Super Sport was designed to reflect the philosophy of its creators, and this has not changed. From Ing. Fabio Taglioni to Ing. Massimo Bordi and Pierre Terblanche, these men have all known Ducati from their youth, and their passion for motorcycles, especially Ducati, has resulted in individual products with a touch of genius.

If there is one word that sums up the Super Sport it is 'desmodromic'. The first Super Sport was the only 750 round-case with desmodromic valve gear, and this has been a significant feature of every Super Sport since. So important has desmo become to Ducati that it is impossible to imagine a Ducati now without this feature.

My own involvement with Super Sports also goes back many years. I still have my first, a 1974 750 that I once rode regularly. With that particular model now assuming classic status, there are other Super Sports that will be ridden in preference, but fortunately even the newest addition, a 900 SS FE, exhibits clear bloodlines to that pioneering 'Imola' replica. Now there is the fuel-injected Supersport, a bike that elevates on-the-road performance to new levels while maintaining strong links with the past.

This is not an uncritical chronicle. Most Super Sports were great motorcycles, but that was not always the case. Various close relatives such as the Mike Hailwood Replicas and S2s have also been included, and my own judgement comes into play when discussing the individual merits of each.

While researching this text I have only

used factory sources, in particular work-shop manuals, owners' manuals, and service bulletins to importers. Some of the earlier information is the result of many years of studying these motorcycles when factory data was less available than now.

As always it would have been impossible to write this book without the assistance of many enthusiasts and individuals around the world. At Ducati the PR department was particularly helpful, not only in unearthing some previously unpublished photographs, but also in finally managing to track down the complete production figures of all the SS Ducatis, published here for the first time. To Silvia Frangipane, Eliana Chieruzzi, Cristina Pitton and Daniela Riberti, many thanks for your support. Others at Ducati who were most giving of their time and information were Ing. Massimo Bordi, who wrote the Foreword, CEO Federico Minoli, Pierre Terblanche, the designer of the new Supersport, Paolo Ciabatti, and Ing. Andrea Forni, principal tester of new Ducatis. Thanks must also go to David Gross and Kristin Schelter, responsible for Ducati Global Imaging, for the use of the Ducati logo and official sanction for this book.

As always there are also many friends and enthusiasts around the world who have contributed photographs and information; in particular Rolf im Brahm, Bruce Finlayson and Phil Schilling have been exceptionally helpful and supportive. Many allowed me to photograph their motor-cycles or use photographs: Steve Atherton, Philip Ayres, Rick Begg, Paul Ison, Paul Jackson, Roy Kidney, Geoffrey Lea, Andrew McCarthy, Andrew Newport, Gerard Porter, Michael Stahl, and Leo Vinci. Don O'Connor of Eurobike Wholesale in New Zealand has always supplied me with the updated Ducati Service Bulletins, vitally necessary for such a work. Finally, the editors of *Streetbike*, Bob Guntrip, *Two Wheels*, Jeremy Bowdler, and *Australian Motorcycle News*, Ken Wootton, allowed access to their photographic archives.

Of course such a work would never be possible without the continued support of my wife Miriam.

Ian Falloon
March 1998

CHAPTER 1

Prelude

The Super Sport story really began when Ing. Fabio Taglioni joined the Ducati company back in the early 1950s. Before Taglioni, Ducati was a government-controlled manufacturer of electronic components and small motorcycles with limited sporting pretensions. While they had set some 50cc records with a tuned *Cucciolo* in 1951, and their pushrod single had grown to 98cc by 1952, by no stretch of the imagination could these be considered designs suitable for the basis of a competition programme. In 1953 the company was split into two divisions, Ducati Meccanica and Ducati Elettrotecnica, and the new General

Without Ing. Fabio Taglioni there would have been no Super Sport. Taglioni has been analogous with Ducati for over 40 years, and every Super Sport bears his mark. Here he is in his office at home in Bologna during 1998, a cutaway drawing of a 1977 900 SS prominent on his drawing-board.

Manager of the former, Dott. Giuseppe Montano, hired Taglioni specifically to develop a new motorcycle to win the *Giro d'Italia*. Ducati had just been humiliated by Laverda in the 100cc class and Montano offered Taglioni the job saying that there would be no pay unless Ducati won the important race the next year.

Fabio Taglioni was born in Lugo on 10 September 1920 and studied at Bologna University, where he graduated after the Second World War. Since 1948 he had been working on a system of desmodromic valve actuation, with a particular application to motorcycles, and this work led him to the successful Bolognese company Mondial, who had recently won three 125cc World Championships. However, it would not be until 1956 that he would see his desmodromic ideas come to fruition. In the meantime Taglioni produced his first masterpiece, the Gran Sport.

The 100cc Gran Sport (affectionately nicknamed the *Marianna*) that appeared in February 1955 was the grandfather of all Ducati sporting motorcycles. Not only did this engine provide the engineering basis that continues through to the present day, but more importantly it also created the sporting ethos now associated with the marque. Compared to the earlier Ducatis, the *Marianna* was very performance-oriented; it was designed primarily to win the all-important Italian street races, and constructed to the highest specifications available at the time. It was also a limited production racing motorcycle, so there were few concessions made when it came to economics.

Looking at the *Marianna* engine it is easy to see how strongly it has influenced nearly all later Ducati designs. The unit-construction vertically split crankcases with finned oil sump and the predominance of ball-and-roller bearings have been a trademark feature of most Ducati engines ever since.

One of the first production sporting overhead-camshaft Ducatis was the 100 Sport of 1958. Strongly derived from the racing Gran Sport, or Marianna, *of 1955, bikes like this were the ancestors of the Super Sport.*

Only the non-Taglioni-designed two-strokes, pushrod singles and parallel twins deviated from the recipe inspired by the *Marianna*. The first production overhead camshaft singles and bevel-gear V-twins shared even more features with the *Marianna*. The single overhead camshaft was driven by a vertical shaft and bevel

gears from the right side of the pressed-up crankshaft. Inside the cylinder head there were two valves, set at an angle of 80°. Of course there were characteristics of the *Marianna* engine that were altered when the overhead-camshaft engine went into production: the cambox was cast separately from the cylinder head, had exposed valve springs, and used straight-cut bevel and primary drive gears. However, the design was so advanced for its day that the basic ingredients were there to influence Ducati engines for decades to come.

What was especially important about the *Marianna* was that Taglioni had designed it for racing on road based circuits, which

would be an area where Ducati would excel in years to come. From the debut of the *Marianna* onwards, all the memorable Ducati successes came on these types of circuit – Montjuich, Imola and the Isle of Man were all road circuits.

In the 1950s success in the *Giro d'Italia* and *Milano–Taranto* was particularly sought after by Italian manufacturers wish-

In 1956 the first successful racing motorcycle with desmodromic valve gear appeared. Ducati's 125cc desmo cylinder head featured three camshafts, two for opening and one for closing the valves. This 1958 example was one of the last constructed and was raced by Mike Hailwood during 1960. Desmodromics would be an essential element of the Super Sport.

ing to increase their penetration of the home market. A few weeks after the *Marianna*'s release it was entered in the *Giro d'Italia* where Gianni Degli Antoni's winning performance in the 100cc class astounded everyone, and the new Ducati set the standard for its class. Soon it had grown to 125cc, and by 1956 175cc. When the 175cc production overhead-camshaft street bikes appeared in 1957 they were strongly based on the *Marianna*. This was another precedent that would feature on production Ducatis in the future; the sporting models would be true race replicas, and that is the essence of the Super Sport.

In the meantime Ducati had decided to enter the world of Grand Prix competition with a 125cc desmodromic racer based on the *Marianna*. The 125 desmo had been particularly impressive at its debut in the hands of Ducati's star rider Gianni Degli Antoni when it won the non-championship Swedish Grand Prix in July 1956. Degli Antoni's tragic death a month later while testing at Monza severely dented team morale and 1957 was spent developing the desmo racer, as well as getting the overhead-camshaft 175cc street bikes into production. When Ducati made their all-out assault on the 125cc world title in 1958, Gandossi only just failed in his attempt to beat Ubbiali's MV for the championship. Ducati may not have won but they had made a significant showing, as well as proving the merits of Taglioni's desmodromic valve gear.

The next year the factory decided not to contest officially the Grands Prix, instead lending a desmo single to the young Mike Hailwood. Hailwood would figure strongly in Ducati history, and he won his first Grand Prix, the 1959 Ulster 125 race, on the little bike. While desmodromics would not figure particularly prominently during the years after the demise of the 125 racers, they would become an essential ingredient in the creation of the first 750 Super Sport.

The *Marianna* was superseded by another pukka racer in 1958, the Formula 3. Also built in limited numbers, it was available in 125, 175 and, later, 250cc versions. While not sharing many components with the production street bikes, the Formula 3 was an important influence on the creation of later sporting Ducati singles, notably the 250 Mach 1 of 1964. Before that, however, the very first Ducati to bear the Super Sport designation appeared in the UK market in 1960. UK bikes carried different names at this time and the 200 Super Sport was a special model derived from the 200 Elite; it offered lighter mudguards, and a range of performance options. Available in the UK until 1965 for those wishing to take advantage of the lower insurance rates for 200cc machines, it was the final 200cc Ducati produced, being by then well and truly superseded by the five-speed 250cc Mach 1. The 67 x 57.8mm engine had a modest 7.8:1 compression ration and produced 18bhp at 7,500rpm. Weighing a mere 111kg (244lb), the performance hardly lived up to the Super Sport label, with a claimed top speed of only 84mph (135km/h).

The next Ducati to carry the Super Sport cognomen was the US-market 250 Mark 3 Super Sport released in mid-1963. The basis of this bike was the four-speed sporting Diana, but now the Super Sport designation gave it genuine production racer status. With a 10:1 compression ratio and a remote float-bowl Dell'Orto SS1 27A carburettor, the 250 single produced 30bhp. Ignition was by a 40-watt flywheel magneto, so the engine could be run without a battery, and it came with a full electrical system. Production racer standing was confirmed by the inclusion of full racing equipment within the Super Sport's specifications. Each Mark 3 Super Sport came with clip-on handlebars, racing mudguards and tyres, and a competition number plate. A year later this Super Sport formed the basis of one of Ducati's greatest sporting motorcycles, the 250 Mach 1. Now with a five-speed gearbox, the Mach 1, and similar US Mark 3, was one of the strongest performing 250s of its day. With a claimed 27.6bhp it was claimed to be capable of 106mph (170.6km/h). The Mach 1 was a Super Sport in everything but name, and a milestone sporting Ducati.

Although there were to be no more

While intended as a racing motorcycle, the Formula 3 also came with full street equipment. This is the 175cc version with an Amadoro front brake, very similar to that of the Grand Prix bikes. Bikes like these did much to establish Ducati as a manufacturer of uncompromised sporting motorcycles.

Ducatis carrying the Super Sport title until 1973, there were still several important sporting models after the Mach 1 that would have a profound influence on the form of the later Super Sports. With the release of the wide-crankcase overhead-camshaft single-cylinder engine in early 1968, Taglioni was able to incorporate a revised desmodromic valve gear set-up using a single four-lobe camshaft instead of the three camshafts that he had employed on the Grand Prix desmo. The resulting Mark 3 Desmo single was the first production motorcycle to feature desmodromic valve gear, the system that would become a feature of every later Ducati Super Sport.

In capacities of 250 and 350cc, the Mark 3 desmo was visually distinguishable from the regular Mark 3 by a 'D' on the side

By 1969 the overhead-camshaft single had grown to 436cc, the range leader being the desmo. These desmo singles were the first production motorcycles to feature desmodromic valve gear, and were the realisation of Fabio Taglioni's dream.

panels and different colours. These early desmos had the unique twin-filler-cap fuel tank, and featured clip-on handlebars without rear-set footpegs. Performance was marginally up on their non-desmo counterparts, but not substantially unless a megaphone exhaust was fitted. The 350 Desmo with the megaphone and Dell'Orto SS1 carburettor had a claimed top speed of 180km/h (112mph). In 1969 the overhead-camshaft single grew to 436cc, and soon there was a 450 Desmo alongside the 450 Mark 3.

From the 450 Desmo emerged a bike of true Super Sport character that unfortunately did not make it into production. Designated the 450 Desmo Superbike, this magnificent machine was closely based on the desmo racer that had been campaigned by Bruno Spaggiari during 1968 and 1969. Looking visually similar to a 450 Mark 3 Desmo, one 450 Desmo Superbike was built during 1970, with the intention of supplying it to special order. Unlike the standard 450 Mark 3 Desmo, the Superbike featured genuine rear-set footpegs to go with the

clip-on handlebars. Instrumentation was limited to the white-faced Veglia tachometer and headlight-mounted speedometer that was usual for this period. Like a Velocette Thruxton, the fuel tank was cut away to allow the fitting of a huge carburettor, in this case a remote-float-bowl 40mm Dell'Orto SS with an open bell mouth. The short Silentium exhaust system was also fairly noisy, and while the dual seat of the 450 Mark 3 was fitted, there were no passenger footpegs.

The engine was considerably modified from standard and included not only the larger carburettor, but also larger valves, stronger crankshaft and connecting-rod assembly, and a higher-compression (10.5:1) piston. Twin-plug ignition was also an option. The running gear also came in for serious attention. The front brakes were twin hydraulic Campagnolo 260mm discs, a radical move in 1970 when not even racing bikes used disc brakes. Suspension was racing Ceriani, 35mm GP forks and twin rear shock absorbers. Borrani alloy rims shod with 3.25 x 18-inch Dunlop KR83

racing tyres completed the specification. With an all-up weight of only 297lb (135kg) including a fairing, the 40bhp (at 9,000rpm) Desmo Superbike was reputed to be good for 120mph (193km/h), an impressive speed for a four-stroke single with street equipment.

Magnificent it may have been, but the 450 Desmo Superbike was unfortunately a victim of timing. Concurrently developed with the 750 and 500 V-twins, Taglioni saw considerably more potential with the new designs, both for racing and the street. While the 500 had moderate success as a pure racer, the 750 would herald a range of street bikes that would eventually form the basis of the entire Super Sport line as we know it.

Undoubtedly the turning point for Ducati

Taglioni's favourite design was the 750 V-twin of 1970, the engine that would form the basis of the classic 750 Super Sport. This is number 750001, and while the bevel gear layout is the same, it has a narrower sump than eventual production versions.

came when Fabio Taglioni was given the go-ahead to design and develop the 750 V-twin. From his first drawings on 20 March 1970, it was a mere four months before a prototype was being road-tested. Towards the end of 1970 several versions of the 750 were constructed and tested, but it was not until July of the next year that the 750 GT was available as a production bike.

With its high handlebars and forward-mounted footpegs, the 750 GT was not exactly a sporting motorcycle, but underneath the touring exterior lay a chassis that was the equal of any other in current production. The frame was Colin Seeley-inspired from experience with the 500 V-twin racers of early 1971, and, like the single-cylinder Ducatis, used the engine as a stressed member. No expense was spared on the suspension or brakes, with special leading-axle Marzocchi forks being developed. Braking was by a single 278mm cast-iron Lockheed front disc brake up front instead of the Fontana twin-leading-shoe drum that had appeared on most of the prototypes. Early 750 GTs used a twin-leading-shoe rear brake, but this soon became a 200mm single-leading-shoe type.

However, it was the engine, and the philosophy behind it, that placed the 750 GT beyond most other contemporary motorcycles. The use of the 90° V-twin engine has since become Ducati's trademark, and it took the competition 27 years to realise that Fabio Taglioni chose it for the right reasons back in 1970! While it was undoubtedly easier for Taglioni to use as much carry-over technology from the overhead-camshaft singles as he could, the choice of the 90° layout was unique. He chose it because it gave perfect primary balance, and the front cylinder could be placed almost horizontally, allowing a lower centre of gravity. Minimal vibration meant that the engine could be solidly mounted in the frame, and with the two con-rods side by side on a common crankpin the engine was not much wider than a single. The downsides were silencing and carburation, particularly keeping the inlet tracts of equal length and of a desired shape.

Another disadvantage was the length of the engine, and the early 750 GT, with its leading-axle forks, had a long 1,530mm (60.2-inch) wheelbase. While less of a problem with street bikes, this would eventually become a limiting factor in racing with the bevel-gear V-twin engine. Steering was also correspondingly slow due to a $29^1/_2$° steering head angle, but the 750 GT was an unquestionably stable motorcycle and provided possibly the best handling available in the larger-displacement class of 1971.

Because it drew heavily on the 350 single, the 750 round-case engine was virtually two cylinders mounted on a common crankcase with a bevel-gear timing chest on the right side. The bevel-gear drive layout was a tribute to Taglioni's engineering purism, but incredibly time-consuming and expensive to manufacture and assemble. While he believes that it was his best design in over 40 years with Ducati, Ing. Taglioni was no economist and it really was quite extraordinary that he managed to get such a complicated engine into production in 1971. It says a lot for the support of the then directors of the company, Arnaldo Milvio and Fredmano Spairani.

It was not only the internals of the 750 engine that were lavishly constructed. The styling and castings of the outer cases were such that the motor was more a part of the aesthetic architecture of the motorcycle than anything else. In so many ways the 750 engine harked back to an earlier era when engines were not compromised by economic or noise limitations, and were a feast for the eyes.

There was no doubt that Fabio Taglioni wanted more from his magnificent 750 than the humble GT. He had purposefully designed the cylinder heads with desmodromic valve actuation in mind, but before that he needed a more sporting variant.

Before the 750 Super Sport there was the 750 Sport. Strikingly styled, a racing-fashion half fairing was available as an option. Essentially a modified 750 GT, the Sport differed from the Super Sport primarily through the use of valve-spring rather than desmodromic cylinder heads.

With such enthusiastic directors, 1971 was a very positive time for Ducati. Soon after the 750 GT went into production a 'Spaggiari Replica', acknowledging Spaggiari's efforts on the 500 V-twin Grand Prix bike, was displayed to Italian concessionaires. While this was essentially a restyled 750 GT, it heralded various prototype 750 Sports that appeared during 1972. When the 750 Sport eventually went into production the 1972 Imola 200 had been run and won, and there was already speculation as to the appearance of the desmodromic 'Imola Replica'. However, while the Super Sport may have been imminent, the 750 Sport was still the only sporting Ducati twin readily available until 1974.

If it had not been for the subsequent Super Sport, the 750 Sport would probably be considered one of the all-time classic Ducatis, but the lack of desmodromic valve gear is the single feature that denies it that ultimate status; however, the sporting ethos was such that it was a true precursor to the 750 Super Sport. Initially with the wide 750 GT frame, by 1973 it had its own frame with a narrower rear subframe. From only a few minor engine modifications the Sport always offered substantially more performance over a 750 GT. Higher-compression (9.3:1) Mondial slipper pistons and unfil-

tered Dell'Orto PHF32 carburettors were the only engine modifications, and the 750 Sport was a surprisingly brisk performer, generally capable of around 200km/h (125mph). Clip-on handlebars, rear-set footpegs and a solo seat completed the sporting profile. There was also the option of a factory half fairing. In other respects the 750 Sport was a close derivative of the 750 GT. Only a single front disc brake was used (although there was always provision for an additional second disc), and a single-leading-shoe rear drum brake. The Borrani alloy wheels were also from the GT, with a WM2 x 19-inch front and WM3 x 18-inch rear.

It was the styling of the 750 Sport that gave it a completely different presence from the 750 GT. The yellow and black colours were complemented by black-painted engine side covers, and even today the 750 Sport is a striking motorcycle. By 1974 the Sport had lost the black engine cases, but remained an uncompromised sporting motorcycle with still only the barest concessions made in the name of civility. Never built in as many numbers as the GT, production was less than 2,000, 856 being produced during 1974. By this time, however, the 750 Super Sport had arrived on the scene, and that is where this story really starts.

CHAPTER 2

The first and the best?

To the dedicated Ducati follower Imola has become a hallowed name, and in Ducati history there is before Imola and after Imola. Before Imola Ducati built interesting but quaintly individual motorcycles. Ducati's first foray into the superbike market, the 750 GT, was such a departure from the British vertical twin or triple, or Japanese four, that it was considered almost eccentric by those outside the enthusiastic Ducati clan, the *Ducatisti*. After Imola all that changed. Ducati could now claim to have taken on the world's best manufacturers and comprehensively beaten them in the big league, Formula 750. The significance of that race win on 23 April 1972 cannot be overestimated. Back in 1956 Taglioni had demonstrated in the Swedish 125 Grand Prix that his unique desmodromic valve gear was a successful idea, but by 1972 that was only a distant memory. After Imola, Ducati was no longer an obscure Italian motorcycle manufacturer, and Imola set the company on the road to the success it has achieved in recent years.

The first Imola 200 was hailed as the Daytona of Europe, a race for production-based 750cc machines rather than Grand Prix motorcycles. With huge publicity and massive prize money it attracted a field that included the best riders and machines available. Multiple world champion Giacomo Agostini was given a special 750cc MV Agusta, which, while it had the shaft drive of the road bikes, sported 500 Grand Prix brakes and suspension. Other entries included works bikes from BSA, Honda, Norton, Moto Guzzi and Triumph, and semi-works bikes from BMW, Kawasaki, Laverda and Suzuki. What this meant was that this inaugural *200 Miglia di Imola* would be a highly publicised and prestigious race, and a win would be a public relations triumph.

For Ducati, Imola was in their back yard, merely 40 kilometres down the A14 *autostrada* towards Rimini and the Adriatic coast. Right from the start Ducati's directors Milvio and Spairani were determined to win this race and they gave Taglioni their full support. Taglioni flew to Daytona in early March to assess the competition, knowing what he was up against. He also knew that Imola was a traditional fast European circuit that placed a premium on high-speed handling rather than sheer horsepower. Recognising that he would probably be out-powered, Taglioni believed that he could still win the race with a better-balanced, and better-handling motorcycle.

Immediately on his return from Daytona, work began on the batch of Imola racers. 750 GT frames with numbers around 751000 were taken straight off the production line, but the engine cases were the early sand-cast type with the extra bolt through the sump for the mounting of the prototype 750 GT's forward footpegs; these cases, pre-engine number 750404, were obviously considered stronger than the later type. So standard were the frames that they retained their centrestand lugs, and during testing before Imola stands were actually fitted! However, the frames were later modified to allow the rider's legs to tuck in more closely, and several versions were tried before the final form was achieved. Only a few weeks later, on 6 April 1972, Franco Farnè took the first 750 racer out to Modena for Spaggiari to test.

While they may have been 750 GT-derived, the Imola racers were true factory racing bikes. Special lightweight fully machined con-rods (weighing approximately 325 grams each) featured dual strengthening ribs around both the big and little ends. The pistons gave a 10:1 compression ratio, and dual-plug ignition was employed to keep the combustion chamber temperatures to a minimum by allowing less spark advance (34°). Additional cooling was provided by an oil cooler mounted on the steering head bracket. The cylinder heads still employed the 80° included valve angle of the standard 750, together with standard valve sizes of 40 and 36mm, but with desmodromic valve actuation. Using a system similar to that of the production desmo single, each camshaft carried four lobes, the valves being operated with polished opening and closing rockers. Unlike the singles, however, much lighter return springs were employed. No alternator was fitted on the right side of the crankshaft, the battery and four-coil ignition being total loss. Taglioni had briefly flirted with Ducati Elettrotecnica electronic ignition on the 500 Grand Prix bikes during 1971, but this had been unreliable so he reverted to points and coils (not Ducati Elettrotecnica) for Imola. Carburation was by new Dell'Orto PHM 40As, also descending from the 500 Grand Prix bikes. The maximum power generated was a modest 86bhp at 9,200rpm at the rear wheel, but with a very wide power band; power dropped to 84bhp at 8,800rpm, 70bhp at 7,000rpm, and 64bhp at 6,000rpm. That 86bhp was certainly a realistic, perhaps even pessimistic, claim, because these bikes were reputed to pull the tallest available gearing, giving 169mph (272km/h).

The Super Sport story started with the Imola 200 victory of 1972, when Spaggiari rode No 9 into second place behind Paul Smart. While these racers were modified 750 GTs, they incorporated many special parts and used early sand-cast engine cases with the extra bolt through the sump.

Straight-cut primary drive gears (31/75) gave a slightly higher ratio (2.419:1) than the 750 GT, and the clutch basket was drilled to save weight. While the standard five-speed 750 gearbox was retained, the kickstart shaft was removed, improving right-side ground clearance. As the only tight right-hand corner at Imola was the famous *Aqua Minerale*, the left megaphone exhaust was high rise, while the front exhaust was tucked closely under the engine side covers. Apart from racing Ceriani shock absorbers, the front forks were 750 GT 'Marzocchi Racing' leading axle, featuring turned-down fork legs with no mudguard mounts. There were other

weight-saving measures, notably a hollow axle and relieved brake disc carriers; however, these bikes were still not exceptionally light for racing machines, with a dry weight of 392lb (178kg). Besides the usual steering head friction damper, a hydraulic steering damper was attached from the front forks to a lug on the frame. Triple disc Lockheed disc brakes were used, but with only left brake callipers available from the 750 GT production run, these were adapted for both front and rear discs, the rear being underslung. A modified front

A few months after the Imola race the first 750 Super Sport prototype appeared, but was never officially displayed. The engine was dominated by the Dell'Orto PHM 40A carburettors, but the bodywork would become that of the 750 Sport.

hub was used at the rear, with a smaller 230mm disc. Both front and rear brake master cylinders featured turned aluminium fluid reservoir extensions.

All-new fibreglass bodywork was designed for the Imola racers, the large fuel tank having wide clear strips moulded into the silver metalflake gelcoat as an instant fuel gauge. As the blue-painted 750 GT-based frame still used the wide rear subframe, the solo seat was also wider than that of the production Super Sport. A small fibreglass front mudguard was attached to the front forks with clamps, and 18-inch Borrani rimmed wheels were used front and rear. The engine breather hose originally hung out from the right side above the shock absorber, but later in 1972 was re-routed through the seat.

Only in the days leading up to the race

had the riders been finalised; obtaining top-flight riders had proved more difficult than Spairani imagined. Renzo Pasolini, Jarno Saarinen and Barry Sheene had already declined offers to ride, but finally Paul Smart was obtained after his wife Maggie accepted in his absence. Smart would partner the 39-year-old veteran Ducati campaigner Bruno Spaggiari, Ermanno Giuliano, and English rider George Dunscombe (sponsored by the British importer Vic Camp). On 19 April 1972 five 750 racers were taken to Modena, still with centrestands, and the following day Smart flew in from the US for more testing. On race day seven bikes were taken to Imola in Ducati's glass-sided transporter: two each for Smart and Spaggiari, one for Giuliano and Dunscombe, and one spare. Another spare remained at the factory in case of an emergency. They were all identical, although Smart's bikes soon had a revised footpeg location to suit his larger frame.

The race itself went almost to plan for Ducati. Both bikes nearly ran out of fuel on the last lap, and, Spaggiari being worst affected, Smart led home for a magnificent 1–2 victory at an average speed of 157.35km/h (97.74mph). Both Ducatis shared the fastest lap with Agostini at 161.11km/h (100.1mph). Spairani was euphoric after this victory, not only presenting the winning bike to Smart, but also promising street versions of the Imola bikes.

Over the next few months the Imola 750s were campaigned around the world as a promotional exercise. In June they went to Daytona, then Mosport in Canada. Smart crusaded his winning bike at various events throughout England in 1972, and one was sent to South Africa at the end of the year, where it was run with reasonable success by Errol James. Spaggiari's second-place bike went to Australia and was raced by Kenny Blake. Unfortunately the factory did not pursue these meetings with the same vigour that they had at Imola. As with just about every factory racer or prototype, those bikes not sent overseas were broken down for spare parts. Taglioni already considered them obsolete and stayed in Bologna working on the next generation of racer. With

new designs on the drawing-board almost immediately after Imola, the 1972 racers were never to repeat the dominance they had so briefly demonstrated.

With Imola out of the way there was time to develop the promised street version of the desmodromic racer. A few months later the first prototype was constructed, but was never publicly displayed. There were important changes to the frame, in particular the adoption of a narrower rear subframe, and this frame would be used on the 750 Sport before the Super Sport and was painted silver on this first example. The blue fibre-glass fuel tank, seat and side covers were also similar to the later 750 Sport rather than the eventual Super Sport. Completing the Sport, rather than Super Sport profile, was the absence of a fairing.

Despite being so obviously Sport-derived, there were still many carry-overs from the Imola bikes. The blue fibreglass front mudguard was taped to the leading-axle Marzocchi fork legs, and 18-inch alloy Borrani wheels were fitted front and rear (a WM2 on the front). The twin front discs were relieved as with the racer, and the hollow axle was also retained, but the front

This early prototype featured twin front discs very similar to the Imola bikes. The brake callipers were Scarab rather than Lockheed, and the leading-axle Marzocchi forks retained their front mudguard mounts.

Also carried over from the Imola racers was the underslung Lockheed rear disc brake.

Only the very earliest 750 GTs featured these clutch covers without an inspection plate. The regulator location was also altered on the production Sport and Super Sport.

brakes were Italian Scarab rather than Lockheed. The underslung Lockheed calliper was still used at the rear, together with a 230mm disc.

For some reason this prototype Super Sport used a very early 750 GT engine. The cases were sand-cast (pre-engine number 750404) with the extra bolt mounting through the sump, just like the Imola bikes, and featured an even earlier clutch cover without an inspection plate. Of course the big change to the engine was the incorporation of desmodromic valve gear and Dell'Orto PHM 40A carburettors. Nothing much happened with this prototype for a few months, but the frame changes became incorporated on the 750 Sport during 1973.

It was not until later in 1972 that another 750 Super Sport prototype was constructed and displayed to the press. Although using the 750 Sport as a basis, this 750 Super Sport had bodywork styled along the lines of the Imola bikes. In addition, the frame (with the narrow rear subframe) was painted blue, and the fibreglass fuel tank,

solo seat, side covers and upper part of the half fairing were silver. As with the Imola bikes, the fuel tank incorporated a wide clear strip in the fibreglass. Black-painted leading axle forks were used, the front mudguard being clamped in place. Another indication that this bike was hastily constructed was the crude fairing-mounted instrument panel that incorporated the Veglia speedometer, a tachometer and an ammeter.

Wheels and brakes also followed along the lines of the racers and the earlier prototype. The 18-inch Borrani rims were shod with Dunlop KR83 and KR84 racing tyres (3.25 x 18 inches), but, late 1972 being a time when Ducati was moving towards Scarab brakes rather than Lockheed, the brakes became Scarab all-round (it was rumoured that Spairani had an interest in the Scarab company, and Scarab brakes continued to be fitted through to 1974, even though he was no longer at Ducati by then). For whatever reason it was a detrimental move, and the Scarab components were never up to the quality of the Lockheed or later Brembo. The desmodromic engine was also 750 Sport-based, with black-painted engine covers. It was only the machined con-rods, desmodromic valve gear and Dell'Orto PHM 40A carburettors that set this prototype Super Sport apart from the Sport. Only one of these 750 Super Sports was constructed, not 25 as has been quoted, and like so many Ducati prototypes it has vanished, company policy always having been (and still is) to break prototypes down into spare parts. This Super Sport was, however, submitted for homologation to the Italian Motor General Management, and the certification number 11871 OM was granted on 9 July 1973. This number would apply to all 750 (and the first 900) Super Sports.

Despite gaining Italian certification,

The 750 Super Sport prototype of late 1972 was really a 750 Sport in disguise. While the style was similar to the eventual production version of 1974, few detail parts were shared.

before production of any Super Sports could proceed there were two things to be negotiated. First was the signing of the notoriously awkward metal-workers' contract that came up for renewal in 1972, and second there was the 1973 Imola 200 race. Taglioni was determined to build the ultimate twin-cylinder four-stroke racer for this meeting. He had originally planned to race at Daytona but had been foiled by the metal-workers' strikes, and it was not until a month prior to the 1973 Imola 200 that serious work began on the new bike.

Unlike the 1972 racer, the 1973 bike shared little with any street Ducati apart from the basic crankcases as required by Formula 750 regulations. The engine used considerably oversquare dimensions of 86 x 64.5mm, which allowed it to rev to around 10,500rpm. There was a narrower, 60° included valve angle, and the overall length of the engine shortened by about an inch. The clutch was a dry multi-plate affair, and the exhausts were now upswept on both sides. A new, more compact frame was designed that had eccentric chain adjusters at the swing-arm pivot, and the swing-arm itself provided three axle loca-

After finishing second at Imola in 1973, Bruno Spaggiari continued to campaign the short-stroke 750s for the next two years. Here is one of the two bikes he had for the 1974 Imola 200 race.

tions for varying the wheelbase.

Shortening the wheelbase was a high priority when Taglioni designed this bike. The 1,530mm (60.2-inch) wheelbase of the earlier bike had limited agility and ground clearance, so the leading-axle Marzocchi forks made way for a centre-axle type, still with 38mm fork tubes. The flat triple clamps of the leading axle forks were retained, however, giving very generous trail and hence stability, at the expense of manoeuvrability. Together with Scarab forward-mounted front brake callipers, these forks would be used on the eventual production Super Sport of 1974. A Lockheed calliper and master cylinder was still used on the rear. Initial runs on the dyno proved disappointing as power dropped off after 9,500rpm. However, in testing Spaggiari reported that the engine revved beyond 10,400rpm, so it was estimated that power was in the region of 93bhp. The complete package was not only more compact, but also considerably lighter at 325lb (147kg).

On 15 April 1973 a crowd of more than 100,000 gathered to watch the *200 Miglia Shell di Imola*. This time, with the race run in two 100-mile legs, it would not be so easy for Ducati. Budget restraints limited the team to three riders, Bruno Spaggiari, Bruno Kneubühler and Mick Grant, and the glass-sided factory transporter looked less full this year with only four bikes in it. Despite being outclassed by Jarno Saarinen on the Yamaha 351, Bruno Spaggiari finished a creditable second overall, with Kneubühler setting the fastest lap in the first leg at 165.147km/h (102.6mph). Undoubtedly the 1973 bikes were an improvement on those of 1972, but Taglioni could see their limitations when faced with increasing two-stroke opposition. There would be no more development on Formula 750 bikes, and for 1974 Spaggiari raced the 1973 bikes at Imola under his own banner, while for the 1975 Imola 200 he managed a team that included Smart and future World 500cc Champion Franco Uncini. These bikes may not have been as significant as the 1972 Imola machines, but they were to exhibit a strong

influence on the production form of the 750 Super Sport.

For 1973 the 750 Super Sport was officially listed on the distributors' price list, but was still not generally available. A few bikes were constructed, however, and three were sent to the United States where one became the famous 'California Hot-Rod' as raced by Cook Neilson and Phil Schilling of *Cycle* magazine (see Chapter 4). A later version was displayed at the Milan Show towards the end of 1973.

Because they used 750 GT/Sport engine and frame numbers, the few Super Sports of 1973 can be considered pre-production, and differed from the 1974 production bikes in a number of details. As the engines were 750 Sport-based they had black-painted engine covers, with lower-crowned rocker covers. Inside, however, they were pure Super Sport. The special machined con-rods featured dual strengthening ribs around the big-end eye, and desmodromic camshafts operated the valves via polished rockers. There were of course the Dell'Orto PHM 40A carburettors mounted on individually welded steel manifolds.

As they were essentially a 1973 750 Sport, these Super Sports used Veglia instru-

The few pre-production 1973 Super Sports featured black engine covers and polished Marzocchi centre-axle forks. The front Scarab brake callipers were generally behind the fork legs. The clear strip in the petrol tank was much wider on these bikes.

ments (with an electronic tachometer), but other parts were specific to them. The Marzocchi front forks had provision for two-bolt attachment of the front mudguard, but with rear-mounted Scarab brake callipers. They were totally unique to these few bikes because the axle still went from the right to the left with the clamping bolt on the right leg. These forks had polished fork legs but black-painted triple clamps. The front 278mm cast-iron discs were also unique to this model, being the solid type fitted to contemporary 750 GT and Sports but with 18 holes drilled in the carriers. The rear 230mm brake was a Lockheed once again, the master cylinder residing beneath the left-side cover, with the calliper underslung. They thus had a very long rear brake hose that was attached to the lower part of the left rear shock absorber to keep it away from the rear wheel.

Cosmetically the half fairing and fibreglass fuel tank with the clear strip were similar to that on the production Super Sport, although a big difference was the greater width of the clear strip and the higher placement of the tank decals. The side covers were still retained by screws on the leading and trailing edge as they were on the early 750 GT and 750 Sport. Certainly only very few of these 1973 750 Super Sports were constructed; one, with the fork legs reversed, was used in some publicity photos and later appeared on the 1995 Super Sport brochure.

Later in 1973 a 750 Super Sport was built for display at the Milan Show. The features of this bike placed it somewhere between the 1973 pre-production bikes and the eventual 1974 Super Sports. The front forks were reversed so that the Scarab callipers were in front of the fork legs,

By the Milan Show of 1973 the 750 Super Sport was approaching its eventual production form, now with polished aluminium engine covers and a revised side-cover attachment.

which were painted black. While the rear Lockheed calliper was still underslung, the engine cases were polished rather than painted black. The clear fuel tank strip was narrower, and the tank decals mounted lower, more in line with the eventual production 750 Super Sports. This bike was submitted for homologation by the FMI (*Federazione Motociclistica Italia*) at the end of 1973, but the statement on this proposal that 100 identical samples had been produced between 2/10/73 and 20/12/73 was obviously untrue; production did not occur until 1974, and only one motorcycle with these exact specifications was built. Some of the specifications quoted on the schedule were also totally different from those of the eventual production Super Sport. The engine featured 'Imola' camshafts with 11mm of intake valve lift and valve timing figures of inlet opening 65° before top dead centre and closing 95° after bottom dead centre. The exhaust camshaft opened the valve 10mm with timing figures of exhaust valve opening 95°

before bottom dead centre and closing 60° after top dead centre. Valve sizes were stated as 42mm inlet and 38mm exhaust, with compression at 10.5:1. With a 24-litre fuel tank the claimed weight was 165kg (333lb). As with much of the information on this sheet, this was also fanciful.

Only a few weeks after the Milan Show, the single batch of 1974 750 Super Sports was constructed, primarily to justify the earlier homologation application. Ducati wanted the bike to be raced in Italian Formula 750 events during 1974, so with no more official racing Taglioni was able to devote his energies to supervising their production. Unlike the earlier prototypes, they were all identical, but as with all-hand assembled machinery there were often detail inconsistencies. A factory technical sheet from 1974 stated that 'the manufacture of the model described (DGM 11871) began on the 2 January 1974 and the minimum set of 200 identical samples was completed on the 10 January 1974.' If this is to be believed they were working very intensely at Borgo Panigale during that period.

All the 1974 Super Sports received a new engine and frame number sequence. The engines had a DM750.1 designation and started at 075001, the '.1' possibly indicat-

When the 750 Super Sport eventually made it into production in 1974, it set new performance standards for production motorcycles, and was styled like no other.

ing that these engines were race-shop assembled. Frame numbers on the 750 Super Sport were DM750SS, and also began at 075001. Because engines were always assembled separately, and prior to installation in the chassis, frame and engine numbers can deviate quite markedly. Finally, access to the official factory production figures for the 1974 Super Sport has ascertained that 401 were built, even though numbers went up to 075411; a figure of 400 safely homologated the motorcycle for two years. Ing. Taglioni was quite adamant that the number was 200 when I asked him about it in 1995, but he possibly meant 200 for both 1974 and 1975, even though there was only one production series.

No longer based on a 750 Sport, the engine of the 1974 Super Sport usually had crankcases with an oil-cooler outlet under the ignition housing between the cylinders. Internally it received a new set of helical primary drive gears with an even higher ratio – 32/70 (2.187:1) – than the 1972

Imola racers. The pistons were the same Mondial three-ring slipper type of the 750 Sport, but the crankshaft and con-rods were special. The latter were fully machined out of billet 16 Ni Cr Mo 12 with a then state-of-the-art computerised milling machine; featuring a dual strengthening rib around the big-end eye only, they weighed about 420 grams each.

The big-end bearings were, however, unchanged, and were still problematic when racing or using extended rpm. As with the 750 GT and Sport, a 36mm crankpin was employed with 18 caged split 5mm roller bearings. The clutch drum bearing sizes were also changed for the Super Sport, now with two Ø25 x Ø47 x 12mm bearings, and the clutch cover had considerably more internal webbing to support the outer bearing. A flywheel was still bolted inside the primary gear. All production 1974 Super Sports had polished aluminium outer engine covers, and the higher-crowned rocker covers that were designed for the 860 with its screw-and-locknut valve adjustment mechanism.

There were new cylinder heads for the Super Sport, not only designed to accept desmodromic valve gear, but also the Dell'Orto PHM 40A carburettors of the Imola racers. These carburettors were unlike later PHMs in that they had round bodies, without provision for choke attachment. The cylinder heads featured inlet studs wider apart (58mm), and, in line with its limited production status, the inlet manifolds were welded steel, not aluminium. Polished rockers operated the 40mm and 36mm valves (still set at 80°) and the desmodromic system was identical to that of the 1972 Imola racers.

Other engine parts were shared with its more mundane siblings, including the five-speed gearbox (six gearbox dogs) and twin points and coil ignition. While the ignition coils on the Super Sport were mounted lengthways under the fuel tank, they were still the weak Ducati Elettrotecnica type

found on the other 750s. With both sets of points mounted on a single plate, setting the ignition timing was also no easier on the Super Sport than the GT or Sport. None of these factors had a detrimental effect on performance, only maintenance; with its desmodromic valve gear, the Super Sport could never be thought of as a low-maintenance motorcycle.

The quality of the valve guides and valve seats was not up to later standards, and the valves needed re-shimming more often on

This must be one of the most original 750 Super Sports in existence. Owned by Brian Dietz it has only covered 33 kilometres from new. (Roy Kidney)

these earlier desmos. A problem facing the owner in 1974 was a lack of sufficient information regarding the desmodromic valve gear. Only a 750 GT owner's manual was supplied with the 1974 Super Sport, and it was not until the following year that factory information was forthcoming. A Super Sport owner's manual came in 1976.

There were even more changes to the chassis. The Verlicchi-built *azzurro metallizzato* (metallic blue) AQ45 steel frame had slightly different dimensions from the 750 Sport (the optional racing exhausts will not fit the Sport), and there were different brakes and suspension. Following the brilliant success of the prototype 860 racer at Montjuich in July 1973, the production Super Sport used an identical set-up. Up front were black-painted 38mm Marzocchi telescopic forks that were totally unique to the 1974 750 Super Sport. While still featuring the two-bolt front mudguard mounts of the few pre-production Super Sports, they had provision for forward

brake callipers, still with the axle going through from right to left. As expected, the triple clamps were the flat type of the 750 Sport. Rear suspension was also Marzocchi, with twin 305mm shock absorbers, the same as fitted to the 750 Sport but with plastic top covers.

Following the example of the 1973 Imola racers there were front forward-mounted Scarab brake callipers, but still a Lockheed on the rear. The Scarab master cylinder on the Super Sport was a leaky and inferior item with a larger (17.5mm) piston than those for the single-disc GT and Sport. While patterned on the Lockheed, the Scarab callipers were also not up to much. The pistons were prone to seizing in the calliper bodies and they all suffered from corrosion. Some Super Sport callipers came with 'SCARAB' engraved on them, some with 'DUCATI', and some with 'MOTOR SCARAB MOZZI'. Most seemed to have 'SCARAB'.

The undrilled front discs were listed at 280mm, but actually measured about 276mm. At the rear was a smaller, 230mm, undrilled disc with a Lockheed calliper mounted above the swing-arm. The Lockheed master cylinder was located beneath the left-side cover, the 1974 Super Sport being the only production Ducati with a rear Lockheed disc brake.

Much of the bodywork and running gear was specific to the Super Sport. Identical wheels with alloy Borrani WM3 x 18 (2.15-inch) RM-01-4777 rims were fitted front and rear, allowing the fitting of the only V-rated tyres available at that time, Metzeler 3.50 Block C7 Racing. They may have been a racing tyre but they were decidedly slippery and the wide flat pattern did not help the slow steering that already characterised the Super Sport. The 18-inch front wheel also gave the Super Sport quite different handling from the other 750s; Super Sports were more stable, with less of a tendency to shake their heads over bumps.

A contributing factor to their handling finesse was probably the mounting of the instruments, headlight and half fairing on a bracket attached to the steering head, reducing steering inertia. All Super Sports had Smiths instruments, mounted on a black plastic panel situated inside the fairing, the cable-driven tachometer having a conservative 8,000rpm redline. The Aprilia handlebar horn and high/low beam switch harked back to the days of the singles, and showed that Ducati cared more about the engine and running gear than ancillaries. The black clutch and brake levers were also more classically rounded than those of later Super Sports; there was something appealing about the basic nature of the controls.

Apart from the rear mudguard, which was a painted 750 Sport item, all the fibreglass bodywork was new for the Super Sport. Painted *alluminio metallizzato* (metallic aluminium), the 20-litre fuel tank was shaped similarly to the Imola racers, with the unique instant fuel gauge of a clear strip moulded into the gelcoat. The width of this stripe (generally 15–19mm) was now much narrower than the racers and earlier prototypes. The solo seat had a zip for access to the rear compartment, and both it and the side cover location were an improvement on the 750 Sport. A narrow (15mm) *azzurro* stripe ran the length of the motorcycle, front mudguard, tank and seat. With plain 'DUCATI' decals with the simple statement 'DESMO', the styling of the 750 Super Sport was classic and timeless.

In all other respects the 750 Super Sport was a pure production racer. Only minimal concessions were made to street legality, and that meant a horn, headlight and tail-light. There was no provision for turn signal indicators, air filtration or proper silencing, and a fully specified racing kit was available on special order. With this kit came a range of rear sprockets, carburettor jets, oil-cooler, racing camshafts (in the famous pink/white and blue/white), racing fairing, and high-rise megaphones.

While the 750 Super Sport formed the basis of many highly successful road racers, as they came from the factory they did not offer a huge performance increase over the

Now considered one of the most desirable of all Ducatis, the 1974 750 Super Sport has timeless styling, complemented by an engine designed to be an aesthetic delight. (Roy Kidney)

750 Sport. On a good day a 750 Super Sport was a 215km/h (134mph) motorcycle, but where it scored was in the poise and balance it offered. The engines were the smoothest of all the 750s, with perfect carburation, and all early 750 Super Sports felt smaller and more compact than their later larger cousins. Much of this was also to do with the weight; while still no lightweight, the round-case bikes were noticeably lighter than the later square-case examples. They were also narrower, with better ground clearance.

After the single batch of 1974 Super Sports, production ceased. Even before the Super Sports were made, the 750 engine, with its complicated camshaft gear drive train, was deemed uneconomic to produce. It was truly an engine from a different era, highly labour-intensive to assemble and full of beautiful, but expensive, machined alloy engine castings. Taglioni had designed this engine to be an aesthetic delight, but even he could not prevent its demise. This left the 1974 750 Super Sport as the only example of the round-case engine with desmodromic valve gear.

Just as the Imola 200 victory of 1972 was a milestone event for Ducati, the 1974 750 Super Sport was the most significant production bike in the company's history. It had every essential ingredient necessary for it to be considered so important. More than any other production Ducati is was a race replica for the street. There were fewer compromises to legislation or economics, and it offered the highest standards of handling and performance available at that time. So well balanced was the 1974 Super Sport that it obviously reflected the genius of its creator, Fabio Taglioni. On top of all this there was a unity about the bike that came from being hand-assembled. Now finally achieving the legendary status it deserves, the 750 Super Sport also fulfilled another important role: from it emerged the Super Sport philosophy, and this launched the Super Sport into the world of series production. In so doing, the Super Sport saved the company from extinction.

CHAPTER 3

860cc and square crankcases

Even before the 750 Super Sport went into production, it was inevitable that a larger version would eventually appear. After the defeat at Imola in 1973 Taglioni decided to turn his attention to the world of endurance racing where his desmodromic twin would not be limited by capacity restraints. So, at the 19th Barcelona 24 Hour race held at the tortuous Montjuich circuit on 7 and 8 July 1973, a specially prepared factory 860cc desmodromic prototype was entered. Ridden by Salvador Canellas and Benjamin Grau, the 860 easily won at an average speed of 113.729km/h (70.67mph), setting a new race record in the process.

This prototype 860 desmo was an amalgam of the 1973 Imola racer and the prototype street 750 Super Sport. The frame was based on the 750 Super Sport (with the narrow rear subframe), but the brakes and suspension were from the 1973 Imola bikes: centre-axle Marzocchi forks with forward-mounted Scarab front brake callipers and an underslung Lockheed disc on the rear. The engine used the early sand-cast 750 crankcases (pre-engine number 750404) with the extra bolt through the sump, and, like the 1973 Imola bikes, a dry multi-plate clutch. It was really a long-stroke '73 Imola racer, using the same 86mm racing pistons. The 60° desmodromic cylinder heads were fed by Dell'Orto PHM 40A carburettors, and as usual for the tight Montjuich circuit, no fairing was fitted.

Later in 1973, at the Milan Show, the Giugiaro-styled 860 GT made its appearance next to the 750 Super Sport. Before the 750 Super Sport even made the production line it was obvious that there were plans afoot to discontinue the 750 round-case engine. When the 860 GT appeared it seemed unlikely that the Barcelona prototype would spawn an 860 Super Sport in the immediate future, and this proved correct. At the 1974 Barcelona 24 Hour race Canellas and Grau again rode an 860 desmo racer, still based on the round-case engine, but this time victory eluded them and they retired after 16 hours while leading.

This year was one of the more difficult in Ducati's history. There were problems with the supply of various proprietary components, as well as managerial uncertainty. Against Taglioni's better judgement both the round-case engine and the overhead-camshaft singles were discontinued, the company putting its faith in the new Giugiaro 860 GT and parallel twins, the development of which stretched the company's resources. Taglioni redesigned the bevel-gear engine (and restyled the cases to mirror the Giugiaro bodywork), but refused to be involved with the parallel twin. By the end of 1974 the 860 GT was the only bevel-twin left in the line-up.

Fortunately there were still those in the company that wanted to race and develop the Super Sport, and they were aided by the

In April 1975 Kenny Blake rode this prototype 860 SS to victory in the Bathurst production race in Australia. It was the only round-case 860 Super Sport.

spectacular failure of the ugly and underdeveloped 860 GT. In early 1975 a prototype 860 Super Sport was dispatched to importer Ron Angel in Victoria, Australia, for Kenny Blake to race at the Easter production race at Bathurst in New South Wales. This was really one of the final 1974 750 Super Sports (it carried engine number 075405) with 86mm racing pistons and a close-ratio gearbox. Visually it was identified by '860 SUPER SPORT' decals on the side covers and rectangular 860 bearing support housings. Blake easily won the 20-lap race, prompting disqualification pending confirmation from the factory that the 860 Super Sport was indeed a production model. By the time this confirmation arrived, the model was in production, but not in the form of Blake's special racer.

One month after the Bathurst race, in May, the sole batch of 1975 Super Sports was produced. As the round-case engine was no longer being produced, these were now based on the square-case engine. What

was surprising was that apart from the engine, the 1975 bikes retained stronger links with the earlier 1974 Super Sport than the 860 GT. It was almost as if the engineers and race department had decided to produce a limited edition Super Sport in spite of increasing legislation. The final form was barely street legal, and could not be sold at all in many parts of the world.

As with the earlier version, the 1975 Super Sport was a limited production motorcycle. Even though engine numbers indicated that 250 750s and 250 900s were built, as with most of Ducati's production some engines were mislaid at some stage (probably during development), and 249 750s and 246 900s were constructed. They were essentially identical, the 750 now using 860 crankcases and being a sleeved-down 900. Despite this, however, the 750 Super Sport continued with the earlier 750 SS engine number sequence, while the 900 SS received new numbers. Still with the DM750.1, the 750 Super Sport had engine

The 1975 Super Sport had a square-case engine derived from the 860 GT, but still the right-side gearshift. This is the 750, virtually identical to the 900.

numbers from 075412 to 075661, while the 900 Super Sport now had the DM860.1 numbered from 086001 to 086250. Frame numbers were, however, shared between the two and continued the DM 750 SS series from 075412. Thus there was no correlation between engine and frame numbers on these bikes, total numbers of the 750 SS being inflated by 250 due to the 900 Super Sport that used 750 SS frames and frame numbers. There was also an anomaly in the 1975 series of frame numbers that had not appeared in 1974. Some frames only had a five-digit number instead of the normal six, the '0' prefix being absent. This appeared at random on both 750s and 900s, but was not significant.

While the running gear was similar to the 1974 Super Sport, the engine was significantly different; there was much more to the 860 re-design than merely an overbore and the square engine covers. The crankcase castings were now a smoother pressure diecasting, and the cylinders 5mm shorter due to shorter forged con-rods (145mm eye-to-eye length). The earlier milled rods had gone, but the new ones, while being slightly heavier at around 440 grams each, were just as strong. They still had the dual strengthening rib around the big-end eye, but in line with the 860 GT they had a smaller, 20mm gudgeon. The 5mm caged big-end roller bearings and 36mm crankpin were unchanged. Forged pistons for both the 750 and 900 were manufactured by Borgo rather than Mondial.

Most of the changes with the square-case engine concerned the bevel-gear drive to the camshafts, and the ignition. The lower bevel-gear layout was completely revised to incorporate an oil-filter and to make the engine easier to assemble. Here Taglioni was very successful, for while some width was added, assembly of a square-case engine with its set of spur gears from the crankshaft was considerably less time-consuming than the round-case. As the oil-filter was now located where the points had previously been located, the Ducati Elettrotecnica ignition for which the 750 engine had always been designed was used. Straight off the 860 GT, this would be one

of the least reliable aspects of the new design, and contributed to premature big-end failure.

Being self-generating, one of the advantages of the ignition system was that when the two green wires from the ignition transducers to the engine stop relay were disconnected, the engine could be run without a battery. Of course this prohibited the use of the lights or horn, but was excellent for production racing. Disadvantages were the savage advance curve that provided a maximum advance of 28° from 1,700rpm. Other problems concerned the mounting of the ignition stator to the inner crankcase wall, where it was subjected to heat and crankshaft vibration. The flywheel now incorporated the ignition magnets and was considerably lighter than that on the 750 round-case. While the Ducati Elettrotecnica ignition facilitated easy starting, as with the 860, it suffered from premature failure.

Elsewhere, the lower part of the engine was pure second series 860 (after engine number 851683), with the same primary drive and clutch (32/70) housing, 200-watt alternator and gearbox. The multi-plate clutch was, however, shared with the earlier 750 rather than the 860 and consisted of eight identical driving plates and eight identical driven plates.

It was the desmodromic cylinder head that set the Super Sport apart from the 860 GT. Both the 750 and 900 received the same desmodromic camshafts, polished valve rockers, welded steel inlet manifolds, and Dell'Orto PHM 40A carburettors. Many of the carburettors were the round-body type that had featured on the 1974 Super Sport, but after supplies of these were used up re-designed carburettors replaced them. These now had bodies with provision for a choke attachment, and some 1975 Super Sports came with one of each type. The 750 Super Sport cylinder heads were differentiated by the '750' camshaft bearing housing, the 900 having the rectangular 860 type. Despite the 900 having a bore increase of 6mm, there was no increase in the valve sizes.

All 1975 Super Sports came specified with the 750-style Conti mufflers, although the exhaust header pipes were new and a smaller-diameter 'R' Conti clamp was used on the header for better sealing; larger-diameter 'M' clamps were still used at the muffler attachment. One of the problems with the installation of the wider square-case engine in the Super Sport frame was that ground clearance was severely compromised, especially on the left where the new exhaust header protruded awkwardly.

Another important difference from the

The clutch side of the 1975 Super Sport. The 750s still used the 750 camshaft bearing housing. The gearshift crossover shaft hole in the clutch cover was plugged.

860 GT was the retention of the right-side gearshift and left-side brake pedal. With the gear selector mechanism still located in the rear right engine cover, any conversion to the left was inevitably going to lead to a loss of feel and accuracy. This was obviously how the engineers felt, too, despite US Department of Transport regulations that stipulated that all motorcycles manufactured after September 1974 to be sold in the United States must feature a gearshift on the left. Selling a few 1975 Super Sports in the US was obviously not a consideration to the engineers at Bologna. The 900s were primarily built for Australian production racing (99 went to Australia), and the 750 for Italian Formula 750 (though 99 of these also went to Australia).

The right-side gearshift and left-side brake necessitated specific levers for this year, as the earlier round-case levers would not clear the wider engine. The kickstart lever in particular was an indication of hasty design somewhere in the development department. If the rider's foot slipped off while starting, the lever could swing underneath, hitting the gear lever and inadvertently selecting first gear. This was not really a problem if the engine did not start, but if it did and the motorcycle was not on the centrestand, it would proceed unexpectedly. Needless to say, this design of kickstart lever only lasted for one year and was not offered as a replacement part.

The kickstart may have been a retrograde step, but the front braking system was vastly improved over the Scarabs of the 1974 Super Sport. The Brembo master cylinder did not leak fluid over the fuel tank and the callipers themselves offered enhanced feel without the problem of pistons seizing in the calliper body. There was also a Brembo rear brake calliper and master cylinder. The Brembo callipers differed from those used on 750s and 860s by having narrower pads and machined faces; they also were without plastic pad covers.

The 900 Super Sports had a blue fairing with silver decals. One of the rarest of all Super Sports, only 246 were built in 1975.

With the Brembo brakes came new cast-iron discs, drilled radially to minimise unsprung weight. The front discs were increased slightly in diameter to 280mm, with the rear being reduced slightly to 229mm. The brake lines were now rubber, with metal pipes to the front callipers.

The important frame dimensions, the $29^{1}/_{2}°$ steering head angle and 1,500mm

wheelbase, were carried over from the earlier model, and the same flat Marzocchi triple clamps were also used, so the steering characteristics were very similar. Other components were also shared with the 1974 model, but the colours were all new. The frame was now painted silver, with the bodywork silver and blue. Whereas the 900 had a blue fairing with silver decals, the 750 had a silver fairing with blue decals. The 20-litre fibreglass fuel tank and solo seat were very similar to the earlier Super Sport, but there was no longer a clear strip in the fuel tank. Already the days of fibreglass fuel tanks were numbered, but again that did not seem to worry those at the factory – Super Sports were still Imola Replicas so they needed an Imola-style tank. Gone were

the old style 'DUCATI' decals, the Giugiaro type taking their place. There was no doubt that the 1975 Super Sport was a styling triumph, somehow managing to blend the hard edges of the square-case engine with the classic Super Sport bodywork. The colours of silver and blue were also inspired, and would carry through with the replacement of the following year.

One of the more interesting features of the 1975 Super Sport was the retention of the 1974 instrument panel and switchgear. While all other Ducatis were moving towards DOT-sanctioned CEV switches, with the ignition switch beneath the fuel tank, the Super Sport was still back in the early 1970s. As with the early 750s the two-position ignition key was between the seat and fuel tank on the left, with one Aprilia horn/beam switch on the left handlebar.

ABOVE *Unlike the touring bikes, 1975 Super Sports used Smiths instruments, instrument panel and switches identical to the 1974 750 Super Sport.*

RIGHT *The 1975 Super Sport was undoubtedly one of Ducati's styling triumphs. Somehow the classic lines of the earlier Super Sport were beautifully blended with the angular 860 engine cases.*

Apart from the Brembo brake lever, the 1975 Super Sport continued with the earlier 750 clutch lever, still black, while the instrument panel with Smiths instruments and headlight switch was identical to that of the 1974 Super Sport. With no provision for indicators (though a flash relay was included in the wiring inside the headlight shell), it was almost as if the designers were trying to tell the legislators something about how sporting motorcycles should be. Somehow the headlight, taillight and horn appeared to be fitted purely as an afterthought.

There were some changes to the running gear for 1975, primarily the brakes and suspension. The wheels, with alloy Borrani WM3 x 18-inch RM-01-4777 rims front and rear, were identical to the 1974 Super Sport, and they were also shod with the

same slippery Metzeler 3.50V18 Block C7 Racing tyres. While the length of the black-painted 38mm Marzocchi forks was unchanged (still with 580mm fork tubes), they had a forward mounting for a Brembo brake calliper, and a four-bolt front mudguard attachment. The rear Marzocchi shock absorbers were slightly increased in length to 310mm and, like the 1974 Super Sport, had plastic top covers. Unfortunately the 5mm increase was not really enough to offset the loss of ground clearance that came with the wider engine and protruding left-side exhaust header pipe. For those more serious about racing a similar racing uprating kit was available for the 1975 Super Sport.

With the more aggressive styling came a stronger-performing motorcycle. On paper the 1975 Super Sport looked to have very similar figures to the 1974 version, but was a noticeably faster machine, with considerably enhanced mid-range power. This became immediately apparent in production racing; where the round-case 750 Super Sport had often disappointed when run in standard trim, the 900 was more than a match for Japanese bikes such as the Kawasaki 900. Unfortunately in the race for which the 900 Super Sport was created, the annual Castrol Six-Hour production race held at Amaroo Park, Sydney, it just failed to win. In the 1975 event, after 5½ hours John Warrian's 900 SS expired with a failed big-end. He had been leading comfortably and, although the moral victor, this was as close as Ducati came to winning this prestigious event. Riding the same 1975 900 Super Sport, Warrian finished fourth in 1977 (with Ron Boulden), and second in 1978 (with Terry Kelly).

Official racing during 1975 was the most serious since the halcyon days of Imola. As endurance racing was the only avenue left where the Ducati twin was still competitive, a fully fledged factory effort contested most rounds. Not only were Ducati competitive, but they almost won the *Coupe d'Endurance* that year. At the first round at Montjuich in July another prototype was ridden again by Benjamin Grau and Salvador Canellas. After a sluggish start,

this time they won comfortably, clocking 11 more laps than their 1973 record in the process, with a winning speed up to 115.456km/h (71.74mph). Grau followed this victory with a similar result at Mugello, now teamed with Virginio Ferrari. With two rounds run it looked to be a Ducati benefit, but unfortunately missing the Liège round, and crashes at the Bol d'Or and Thruxton, ruined Grau's chances and he eventually finished third in the championship. Only the best three finishes were counted in the final standings, and two wins were just not enough.

By now the factory racers were considerably removed from any street derivative, and more closely related to the 1974 750 SS than the later square-case. These endurance bikes displaced 905cc (with 88mm pistons) and still used the round-case bevel-gear set-up. The crankcases, however, were specially cast to enable the exhaust pipes to tuck in much more closely and use low pipes rather than the high-rise Imola type. Links with the earlier 1974 Super Sport continued with the brakes and front forks, forward-mounted Lockheed and, later, Scarab brake callipers. Initially regular Borrani alloy-rimmed wheels were used, but by the end of the season these had been replaced by magnesium Campagnolo. It seems surprising that the racing bikes were still using Scarab components long after the street bikes had switched to Brembo. Perhaps less surprising was the continued use of the round-case motor as the basis for the racers, and this was also to feature on most of the subsequent NCR bikes. Taglioni felt that he had to compromise his design when he re-designed it for the square-case, so all factory endurance racing Ducatis were round-case based.

Despite being a less pure design, the square-case engine still offered some significant advances over the round-case. The entire bevel-gear layout was better supported and far easier to set up for correct meshing and backlash. The addition of an oil-filter, even though only a bypass type, was an advantage. In other respects, too, the 1975 Super Sport was an improvement over the classic 1974 version. It

certainly had better brakes and a more powerful engine, but unfortunately the ignition and big-end marred what was still one of Ducati's finest ever sporting machines. Even with so few examples built, the 1975 Super Sport (both 750 and 900) has become overshadowed by its more glamorous round-case brother.

Yet these Super Sports were also the last pure sporting motorcycles available anywhere built regardless of current or impending legislation. Arguably amongst the best styled Ducatis ever, the 1975 Super Sport still looks good nearly 25 years on. In

An unrestored 1975-model 900 Super Sport. The indicators are non-standard, as are the shock absorbers. A wonderful motorcycle and the epitome of the words 'Super Sport'.

1975 it was the only shining star in the rather bleak landscape of Borgo Panigale, its importance only emphasised by the spectacular failure of the 860 GT and parallel twins. For the next year the Super Sport would be softened and put into regular production, leaving the 1975 versions as unique examples of uncompromised sporting motorcycles.

CHAPTER 4

Compromise

The transition from 1975 to 1976 was one of the more difficult periods for Ducati. After putting their blind faith in the flawed 860 GT, management did a quick about-face to sanction the release of the more appealing 860 GTS. This model brought some significant improvements, but, more importantly, it created a change in emphasis for the company, a movement back to motorcycles with a more sporting focus.

As the 1975 Super Sports had been constructed without regard to any present or future regulations in most countries, and in such few numbers, it seemed that they would be the last of their breed. What happened next was therefore totally unexpected. The Super Sport had been so successful in those few countries where it could be sold that dealers in other countries wanted it too. While 860s sat languishing in showrooms, dealers wanted Super Sports. Fortunately, for once Ducati listened and it was decided during 1976 to put the Super Sport into regular production; this would mean modifications to enable it to pass various regulations, but in so doing the Super Sport became the lynch-pin in the Ducati line-up.

In the meantime the management of Ducati's then owners, EFIM, decided to pull the plug on official involvement in racing. While tacitly supporting NCR (Nepoti Caracchi Racing), Ducati still contested the *Coupe d'Endurance*, but after the near success of 1975 their two 905cc racers failed to win a single event. The bikes were too fragile, and the budget not big enough to compete with the giant well-supported French endurance teams. Fortunately for Ducati, they still had a team of enthusiastic engineers and mechanics prepared to work after hours to keep the Ducati name alive on the racetrack. Not only was Taglioni directly involved, but also senior factory mechanic Franco Farnè. The NCR team was completed by Mario Recchia and Piero Cavazzi.

It was some time after the 1975 Super Sports had been built that a replacement production prototype appeared. First sent out to Australia for evaluation in July 1976, this was initially a modified 1975 Super Sport. A 900 SS, it had a blue rather than a silver frame, and there were several 1975 features, particularly an earlier Tommaselli throttle and kickstart lever. In most other respects, however, this bike paved the way for the production Super Sport of 1976 and 1977.

Meeting road registration requirements anywhere in the world required air-cleaners, turn signal indicators, and quieter mufflers. British legislation called for a steel fuel tank rather than fibreglass, and US regulations a left-side gearshift with a one-down, four-up pattern. To the purist comparing it to the 1975 version it may have seemed over-sanitised, but underneath there were few serious changes. When it finally made the production line in September 1976, the Super Sport not only met all these regulations, but the soul of the motorcycle was preserved.

Whereas the 1975 Super Sport production had been split 50/50 among 750 and 900s, the 900 now became the major partner; the 750 Super Sport was still available but in far fewer numbers. Only 220 750 Super Sports were constructed in 1976, while 900 production increased to 1,020 in 1976, with a further 633 in 1977. To have the 900 homologated as a separate model it now received its own frame number sequence, although engine numbers continued from before; thus engine and frame numbers were always approximately 250 apart. The same applied to the 750 Super Sport, which continued to use both the earlier engine and frame number sequences. Engine numbers for the 900 Super Sport began at DM 860.1 086251, soon moving into the 087 series. As series production took over, the '.1' designation disappeared, but remained on the 750 Super Sport through until 1978. Only the first 280 1976 900 Super Sports received the '.1' designa-

tion, these being the last of the official 'homologation' series. The 1976 frame numbers for 900 Super Sports began at DM 860SS 086001, the 750 Super Sport continuing on from DM 750SS 075911, while the latter's engine numbers continued from DM 750.1 075661.

Within the engine there were only minor changes from 1975 specifications. The kick-start gear became 36-tooth to improve the starting ratio, and the clutch housing and inner clutch drum were now the same as the 860 GTS (third revision, from engine number 852178) with two differently sized bearings. The clutch plates, however, were still as with the 1975 Super Sport, with no bent tabs. Initially the 1976 Super Sport retained the polished valve rockers, but with the loss of the '.1' engine number these

Most of the changes to the Super Sport for 1976 were to enable it to comply with legislation around the world. This 900 originally had turn signal indicators and would have left the factory with 32mm Dell'Orto carburettors and Lafranconi mufflers.

soon became the regular forged type. The Ducati Elettrotecnica ignition was retained, and there were no changes to the crankshaft or big-end bearings, which meant that the 1976 and 1977 Super Sports suffered the same reliability problems that had afflicted the 1975 models. As with the 1975 versions, 750 Super Sports were sleeved-down 860s, the only visual difference being the round-case 750 camshaft bearing covers.

There were also few changes to the basic chassis and running gear, the wheels, brakes and suspension being largely carried over from 1975, as were the important frame dimensions. Tyres were now Pirelli Gordon MT18 Super Sport, an improvement on the Metzelers. Where it really mattered the Super Sport was left untouched, the changes really having little effect on the function of the motorcycle. Importantly, the Super

Moving the rear brake to the right side meant that the master cylinder was now exposed. From 1976 onwards there were also new footpegs and a revised kickstart lever.

Sport still used the 750 GT as a basis rather than the 860 GT.

The first items to disappear from the earlier model were the Dell'Orto 40mm carburettors and Conti mufflers. Taking the Dell'Orto PHF 32A carburettors with individual air-cleaners and chokes and the Lafranconi mufflers from the 860 GT and GTS certainly made the motorcycle quieter and slower, but not excessively. The biggest problem was the look of the mufflers. Even on the 860 they had looked ugly, and on the Super Sport were decidedly out of place. Fortunately the 40mm carburettors and Contis were always available as an option, often even coming in the crate with the 900 Super Sport. All the Dell'Orto 40As now had bodies with provision for a choke attachment, but still came with tickler buttons. As the production moved from limited to series, the welded steel inlet manifolds made way for regular cast aluminium. The Conti mufflers were also altered and had a longer and larger bracket, still effective but not quite as attractive as the earlier type.

To comply with US regulations the gearshift needed to be moved to the left. This was done in the same way as with the 860 GT, via a shaft at the rear of the engine, the gear selector mechanism still residing in the right-side rear engine cover. Requiring new levers and footpegs, the gearshift conversion was probably the least satisfactory aspect of the 1976 and 1977 Super Sports, the addition of an extra linkage leading to a sloppy gearchange that deteriorated over time. The footpeg arrangement, too, was less satisfactory than the earlier type, the pegs attaching to brackets bolted to the frame rather than welded lugs. The pegs were, however, now folding with rubber footrests.

As the gearshift was on the left, the rear brake needed to be moved to the right. Both the rear Brembo master cylinder and electronic regulator were relocated, the master cylinder now on the frame muffler bracket and the regulator beneath the right-side cover. The angle of the muffler bracket was altered to allow for the master cylinder, and this is the easiest way to identify visually a later Super Sport frame. The front master cylinder was also altered to incorporate a clear plastic fluid reservoir, and with this came a reshaped body so that the master cylinder could fit closer to the handlebar.

When it came to the bodywork and ancillary components, just about everything was new for the 1976 version. No longer was the 20-litre fibreglass Imola-style fuel tank fitted as standard, but a steel 18-litre 750 Sport-style tank used instead. The fibreglass tank was, however, always listed as an option, and the frame featured the wider bracket attachments required for the larger tank. With the steel tank came new decals, the 'DUCATI' being blue. As the tank was shorter there was a new solo seat, this also incorporating a plastic crankcase breather catch tank that then connected to the front air-cleaner box. A dual seat was also an option, further compromising the single purposefulness of the 1975 Super Sport. The steel tank was undeniably safer and more practical but lacked the elegant grace of the 'Imola' tank.

Complementing the steel tank was a new fairing, similar to before but slightly narrower and taller. There was also a taller plexiglass screen and cut-outs to provide for indicator stalks with Aprilia indicators; these were not the neatest attachment, but a necessary evil. While European-specification models continued to use the same Aprilia 60/55-watt halogen headlight and small 750-style taillight, US 900 Super Sports had an Aprilia sealed-beam headlight and larger 860 GT-style taillight. As for 1975, the 750 Super Sport fairing was silver with blue decals, and the 900 Super Sport blue with silver decals.

There were new handlebars, switches and instrument panel for 1976. The clip-on handlebars were designed for regular production so no longer had the individually welded Allen bolt attachments. While the Smiths instruments were still used on US bikes, some European-specification Super Sports during 1977 featured Veglia instruments, similar to those used on earlier 750 Sports, but the tachometer had an 8,500rpm redline. The black plastic instrument panel now incorporated the ignition switch (three positions rather than the earlier two), as the light switch moved on to the handlebars to be incorporated in a new Aprilia switch. It was interesting that Ducati still used an Aprilia handlebar switch on the Super Sport while CEVs appeared on all the touring models. This would not be for long, however, and during 1977 many Super Sports were fitted with a new type of CEV switch. The metal Tommaselli throttle now had the throttle stop screw mounted underneath the throttle body.

While all these small changes were primarily to appease either the bureaucrats or accountants, fortunately the function of the Super Sport remained unimpaired. With the Dell'Orto 40mm carburettors and Conti mufflers the performance was restored, and with the fibreglass fuel tank the 1976 Super

OVERLEAF *Far fewer 750s than 900s were constructed from 1976. The earlier Imola-style fuel tank fitted here was always an option, and these Super Sports originally had turn signal indicators.*

Sport even shared the earlier version's rakish styling. The only area where the 1976 Super Sport really suffered in comparison was in the gearchange.

As production moved into 1977 there were few changes. The 750 Super Sport continued, still on a much smaller scale than the 900, while the latter was geared for entry into the US market, albeit still in relatively small numbers; 357 were sent there during 1977. It would be the first sporting Ducati in the US since 1974, and its release would have been relatively insignificant but for the Daytona Superbike race in March 1977, one of Ducati's most important victories over the years. While Imola may have set the scene for Ducati in Europe, it meant little in America; Daytona has always been the important race in the US, and the win was crucial for Ducati's fortunes there.

The story of the 'California Hot-Rod' had actually begun at Imola in 1972. Phil Schilling was sent to cover the race for *Cycle* magazine and afterwards, when Spairani had promised production replicas, Schilling said, 'Put me down for the first.' It took a while for the 'first' to arrive, and it was one of the three 1973 pre-production 750 Super Sports that went to the United States. After appearing on the cover of Schilling's book *The Motorcycle World*, it was raced by *Cycle* editor Cook Neilson in the 750 class during 1975. Subsequent development saw it become the 883cc 'Overdog' racer that Schilling tuned and Neilson raced in the AMA Superbike series of 1976 and 1977. The culmination was the victory at Daytona in 1977.

With little factory support Schilling and Neilson developed their round-case 750 Super Sport into what was one of the fastest bevel-gear Ducati twins ever. Timed at 149.5mph (240.6km/h) through the speed trap, they completely dominated the 50-mile race, winning at an average speed of 100.982mph (162.51km/h). Once again the Taglioni recipe for a racing motorcycle had been vindicated. With only 90.4bhp at 8,300rpm on tap, the 'California Hot-Rod' certainly was not the fastest in the race, but provided the best balance between power and handling. In an era where Superbikes were predominantly overpowered engines in flexible street chassis, the Ducati showed that it was essentially a racing chassis that had been modified for the street. Nicely summed up by Schilling as 'not bad for a couple of amateurs', this win, coupled with the publicity in *Cycle* magazine, established the Super Sport on the US scene as a serious sporting motorcycle.

Meanwhile in Europe the NCR-prepared Ducatis again contested the *Coupe d'Endurance*, but again without success. That Neilson and Schilling were successful without factory support while the NCR bikes, with considerable factory resources to draw on, could make no impression, really puts the scale of the *Cycle* victory into perspective. By 1977 the NCR Ducatis not only had narrow crankcases and dry clutches, but also 60° cylinder heads, factory camshafts and crankshafts, and multitudes of special chassis parts. The only non-race kit parts that Schilling and Neilson managed to obtain were racing crankshafts with the lightweight dual-rib con-rods, and a close-ratio gearbox. After the race win the factory sent out a set of 60° cylinder heads, but by that stage they had decided to retire the bike; it was sold to Dale Newton and subsequently raced by Paul Ritter. All their development was done in America, involving Jerry Branch cylinder heads with 44mm Harley-Davidson XR750 inlet valves, and a gearbox by Marvin Webster, more noted for gearboxes for Indianapolis race cars.

While the quasi-factory racers struggled in the *Coupe d'Endurance*, 1977 brought a new racing formula that promised to follow on where Formula 750 had initially intended so much – that was before the Yamaha TZ750 took over. As compensation for the Isle of Man losing its Grand Prix status, and thus being a World

One of the most famous racing Ducatis, the Cycle *magazine 'California Hot-Rod' that Cook Neilson rode to victory in the 1977 Daytona Superbike race. Although based on a pre-production 750 SS, this bike did much to promote the Super Sport in America. (Bruce Finlayson)*

Championship event, three new races were run at the 1977 TT, the TT Formula 1, TT Formula 2 and TT Formula 3, and each came with a World Championship on offer. Like Formula 750 in its early days, TT Formula 1 looked tailor-made for Ducati, four-strokes from 500 to 1,000cc competing with two-strokes up to 500cc, but with street bike homologated engine castings. Choice of chassis, suspension and fuelling system was up to the manufacturer, which meant that the NCR Ducatis, with their light chrome-molybdenum Daspa frames and special Marzocchi suspension, were eligible.

Production of the 750 Super Sport continued into 1977 on a reduced scale. All had a solo seat, but non-standard features of this 1977 model include the 'Imola' fuel tank, wheel rims, no indicators, and footpegs and levers. The fairing-mounted mirrors were a factory option from 1978.

In the 1977 TT Formula 1 race Roger Nicholls on a Sports Motorcycles-entered 860cc NCR Ducati was the moral victor after the race was shortened by one lap due to appalling conditions. Honda had an advance whisper so dispensed with their last-lap stop, allowing Phil Read to win by 39 seconds. However, Ducati would get their revenge in 1978 (see Chapter 6).

Only a few minor changes needed to be made to the European 1976 900 Super Sport to meet US requirements. With the sealed-beam headlight came a revised wiring loom and three-fuse fusebox, a system that followed that of the 860 GTS, which had already received three different versions. It took the engineers some time to settle on an effective electrical system for the square-case engines and it was not until later in 1977 that most of the problems were resolved. There was another instrument panel, now with five warning lights, additional lights being provided for indicators and neutral.

The left-side switch block now became CEV, and this would feature on all Super Sports until 1981. US 900 Super Sports also received an additional engine stop switch that clamped on to the right handlebar. The front indicator attachment was altered, and this would also become standardised on later Super Sports. There were no alterations to the frame, brakes or suspension from 1976, but Michelin M45 tyres were fitted for 1977, a 3.50V18 on the front and a 4.25/85V18 on the rear.

During 1977 100 750 Super Sports were made. They looked identical to the 900s except for the fairing colours and 750 camshaft bearing supports, but as they were all European specification, they used Aprilia switches and Veglia instruments. Engine and frame numbers were still in the 075 series, indicating the few numbers of these bikes now constructed. They were now built primarily for Italian 750 racing (hence they all came with a homologated solo seat). However, with the price being very similar to the 900, most distributors did not bother to stock the 750 and it was generally only available in Australia and Germany.

The 900 Super Sport of 1977 was virtually unchanged from 1976. This US specification 1977 900 would have left the factory with 32mm Dell'Orto carburettors and Lafranconi mufflers. (Roy Kidney)

Even as the 1976 Super Sport was being developed for series production, moves were under way to rectify some of the problems that had afflicted the early square-case engines. It was at the Bologna Show at the end of 1976 that the prototype Leopoldo Tartarini-designed 900 Sport Desmo Darmah was first displayed. This still used the earlier engine with the gearshift crossover shaft and Ducati Elettrotecnica ignition, but further developments were waiting in the wings. Less than one year after series production of the Super Sport had commenced, the 900 Sport Desmo Darmah was released. Now incorporating significant engine and electrical improvements, it would be only a matter of time before these filtered through to other models. The next series of Super Sport promised to overcome the criticisms of sloppy gearshift, premature big-end failures, and unreliable ignition.

CHAPTER 5

Fashion
over function

The gradual transition of the 860 GT through the GTS to the Darmah was a tribute to the development skills of Fabio Taglioni and his engineering team. In the space of two years, not only was the reliability dramatically improved, but also the motorcycle became more refined. It took a little time for most of these improvements to appear on the Super Sport, but when they did they were well worth the wait. The 1978 900 Super Sport, while being more civilised than the earlier versions and lacking some of the naked aggression, still retained that pure sporting character. This was largely because the engine made no less power and the chassis was left untouched.

Very similar visually to the 1976–77 900 SS, there were some important improvements for 1978. Fortunately none of these affected the function of the Super Sport and it retained its sporting focus.

As before, the Super Sport carried little excess baggage. With the redesign of the engine came most of the improvements to the electrics and gearshift that had appeared on the Darmah. Surprisingly, however, while the 900 Super Sport featured a number of significant alterations, the few 750 Super Sports available in 1978 were left-overs from the previous year. With DM 750.1 engines, they still had Ducati Elettrotecnica ignitions, the crossover gearshift and earlier footpegs. Engine numbers were in the 075800–900 series, with frame numbers entering the 076 series. Other ancillary parts, such as instrument panel and switches, were shared with the 1978 900 Super Sport.

While the 1978 900 Super Sport looked visually similar to the 1976–77 version, underneath there were some genuine improvements. Engine numbers had by now reached the late DM 860 087000 series and soon moved into the 088001 sequence. Production was also up from 1977, with 1,037 built in 1978. It had taken some time, but finally the crankshaft and big-end bearings were redesigned. Following on from the Darmah, the big-end bearings were now 23 caged 3mm needle rollers on a 38mm crankpin, giving more bearing surface area. Until engine number 088026 a 36/38mm stepped crankpin was used, but from 088027 a straight 38mm crankpin was employed. While this modification may not have made the Super Sport unbreakable, service life was increased markedly. Premature big-end failure was probably the major problem afflicting the earlier 860s (always more so than the 750s) and this new bearing set-up restored reliability to at least acceptable levels.

Complementing the new big-end bearings was a totally revised ignition system and redesigned gear selector mechanism, also from the Darmah. Contributing to the improved service life of the bottom end, the new Bosch ignition may not have been perfect but it was much better than the Ducati Elettrotecnica that always seemed to expire when least expected. Functionally, the biggest improvement came with a far gentler ignition advance curve. The ignition rotor was shaped so as to provide four stages of advance. At 900rpm advance was 9°, going to 16° at 1,800rpm and 28° at 2,800 rpm. The maximum of 32° advance was progressively reached at 4,000rpm. As the system was no longer self-generating the engine could no longer be run without a battery. Gradually the maximum ignition

1978 saw the Super Sport gain the engine improvements of the Darmah of 1977. There was a new clutch cover that incorporated the ignition pick-ups and a superior left-side gearshift. This is a late 1978 750 SS, almost identical to the 900 except in capacity and the colour of the fairing.

advance had been reduced from the 35–38° of the 1975 900 Super Sport, and the 1977 900 Super Sport had specified 32–34° advance. The 750 Super Sport remained at 34–36°, indicative of the extra stress placed by the larger pistons on the big-end assembly.

With the ignition pick-ups no longer mounted on the crankcase wall but inside the clutch cover, a 750-style external flywheel was used. Until engine number 088318 this was the heavy round-case 750 GT/Sport/Super Sport type, but from 088319 the flywheel was narrower and lighter. An ignition rotor bolted on to the end of the crankshaft. The ignition pick-ups ran in the engine oil, which was not the perfect solution as the wires and connections suffering from oil contamination over long periods. On the right side of the crankshaft the alternator became the revised 900 SD type, still 200 watts.

New engine cases were shared with the 900 SD Darmah. The left crankcase no longer had a plug for the ignition wires under the front engine mount, all the ignition leads being included in a new engine

The footpeg and lever set-up was also revised for 1978, the folding steel footpegs similar to those of the 1974–75 Super Sports.

clutch cover. This also now had an extra plug for ignition pick-up inspection. Internally there was the revised Darmah gearshift and selector mechanism now properly located on the left side behind the clutch basket. The primary drive gears and clutch were also the same as the 900 SD. Rather than eight identical driving and eight identical driven discs as on all the previous Super Sports, there was now one inner driven disc with bent tabs, and an outer driving disc with the bent tabs facing inwards. The rear right-side engine cover was also shared with the Darmah and had no internal selector adjusting components; it was easily recognised by not having any external adjustment mechanism or selector shaft. There were only minor changes in specification to the cylinder head. New O rings, with a different heat grade, were used in the valve guides, and the camshaft bearing supports were the less angular 900 SD type.

As with the 1977 Super Sport, all 1978 versions (750 and 900) came standard with the Dell'Orto PHF 32A carburettors with individual metal air-filter boxes, and Lafranconi mufflers. The Dell'Orto 40A carburettors with ticklers, and long-bracket Contis were still specified as an option. It was as though Ducati were apologetic for

the way they had to subdue the Super Sport to meet the increasingly stringent noise and emission requirements, not only in America, but also in Europe.

The other improvement over the 1976–77 Super Sport was a by-product of the gear selector mechanism now being incorporated under the clutch housing on the left side. As the crossover shaft was no longer required, completely new levers and pedals graced the 1978 900 Super Sport. Reminiscent of the metal footpegs of the 1974–75 Super Sport, these were folding, and with a finer metric thread. The new rear brake and gearshift levers were aluminium rather than the earlier chromed steel. In a uniquely late 1970s Ducati touch, one end of the rear-set gearshift and brake linkages had a usual sloppy clevis pin, while the other end a ball joint.

There were no changes to the specification of the black-painted 38mm Marzocchi forks or Brembo brakes. The early 08 callipers, with machined bodies and thinner pads, were still used at this stage, as were the drilled 280mm and 229mm discs. While the 310mm Marzocchi shock absorbers with black springs were also the same, they had new bushes and silent-blocs. In line with that being fitted to the Darmah, the front axle no longer had the Tommy bar on

the right, but accepted a 17mm spanner.

There was yet another change to the instrument panel for 1978 (fourth version). Miles-per-hour instruments were still Smiths, but all kilometres-per-hour instruments were Veglia (240 kilometres per hour), with a mechanical tachometer (redline 8,500rpm). Like the previous version, the fourth Super Sport instrument panel now had five warning lights, but these were arranged differently. As before, the panel also located the three-position ignition key. The handlebars, metal Tommaselli throttle with the throttle stop screw underneath, Verlicchi handgrips, and black brake and clutch levers were unchanged from the 1977 version.

The left-side handlebar switch block was the same CEV unit from 1977, and the wiring loom similar to that on the final 900 GTS. As with the latter, the European-specification headlight changed from an Aprilia to a 55/60-watt halogen CEV. This had a differently shaped headlamp rim and had the usual plastic beading to seal it in the fairing. The flash relay was mounted under

The fourth version of the Super Sport instrument panel also appeared in 1978. This basic design would continue through until the demise of the bevel-gear SS in 1982.

the seat with the three-fuse fusebox, but there was now no engine stop relay except for US bikes. The single *Belli* horn was still fitted, but relocated in front of the left front downtube to allow the fitting of the two Bosch ignition coils.

Following on from the US-specification 900 Super Sport of 1977, all the taillights were standardised to the larger CEV lens on the chromed metal bracket. The front and rear indicators were still CEV, but now came from the 900 SD. Also in line with the US 900 Super Sport, there was an alteration to the mounting of the front indicators.

Because the steel fuel tank and decals were also the same as the 1976–77 Super Sport, the two bikes looked superficially similar. Most 1978 900 Super Sports came with a dual seat with a lockable toolbox, although the single seat was always available as an option. There was also a slight change to the front mudguard shape, now having a more rounded profile. The tyres fitted to the Borrani alloy-rimmed wheels were still Michelin M45, 3.50V18 and 4.25/85 x 18.

The 1978 900 Super Sport possibly represented the epitome of Taglioni's design. Still painted the classic blue and silver, and with the Borrani alloy-rimmed wheels, they also offered improved reliability and refinement. Any Super Sport with Bosch ignition has quite a different feel but gives nothing away in performance. Consequently, while not so many were manufactured, these 1978 900 Super Sports (and the later 1979 750 Super Sports) were the last to retain close links with the silver Imola racers.

It was inevitable that fashion would enter into the Super Sport equation at some stage, and by 1978 spoked wheels with alloy Borrani rims looked decidedly old-fashioned. The Darmah had featured cast alloy wheels since mid-1977, so it was only a matter of time before these would appear on the Super Sport. Because the NCR racing

One of the 30 late 1978 750 Super Sports, the final Ducatis with Borrani alloy wheel rims. They were magnificent motorcycles, possibly representing the bevel-drive Super Sport at its zenith.

Ducatis had also been using magnesium Campagnolo wheels since 1976, it was inevitable that the 900 Super Sport, as Ducati's race replica, would inevitably follow suit. In retrospect they offered no advantage over the Borranis, and in reality were initially functionally inferior.

The first production 900 Super Sport to feature cast alloy wheels appeared at the Le

Mans 24 Hour race on 22–23 April 1978. In a non-championship event held on the 4.24-kilometre Bugatti circuit, Benjamin Grau and Salvador Canellas rode a factory-prepared production 900 Super Sport to victory in the Silhouette class. They finished a creditable fifth overall, behind fully fledged Honda RCB 1,000cc endurance racers. Running air-cleaners and Contis,

Ducati stalwarts Grau and Canellas showed that the 900 Super Sport was still a convincing production racer. While the win in the Isle of Man TT Formula 1 race (see Chapter 6) was undeniably the most momentous result for Ducati during 1978, this win in the Silhouette class was also significant.

Evidence of the increasing importance of the British market to Ducati was shown

when the first version of a pre-production 900 Super Sport with alloy wheels was displayed in the UK during June 1978. Painted black and gold, this special British edition 900 Super Sport had decals that differed from the eventual production black and gold 900 Super Sports and did the rounds of magazine road tests. Black Super

The black and gold 900 Super Sport of 1979–80 was designed to appeal to British bike enthusiasts and created with the British market in mind. Single seats were still an option and the shock absorbers on this example are non-standard. (Geoffrey Lea)

Sports generally became available during 1979, with decals patterned on the blue and silver bikes.

Interestingly, while the 900 Super Sport was changing over to cast alloy wheels, a small number of 1979 model year 750 Super Sports, still with Borrani alloy rims, were built in late 1978. In most respects they were identical to the blue and silver 1978 900 Super Sport, but with the usual 750 Super Sport fairing colours, silver with blue stripes. These few 750 Super Sports were not officially listed in any advertising or factory documentation but were all identical. Only 30 were built, and they were one of the more interesting Super Sports.

These final 750s now followed the 900 Super Sport example by losing the '.1' engine number designation, and had engine numbers in the late DM750 075900 series. Frame numbers were about 250 ahead as expected, and in the DM 750 SS 076200 range. As these were the final 750 Super Sports, total production from 1974 until 1979 (round- and square-case) was exactly 1,000 examples, by far the fewest being at the end of the production run.

The engine specifications also followed those of the 1978 900 Super Sport, with Bosch ignition and the Darmah-style left-side gearshift. These engines used the crankshaft with the 38mm crankpin and 3mm caged roller big-end bearings. As with other square-case 750 Super Sports, the only external distinguishing feature between the 750 and 900 was the '750' camshaft bearing support. All these last 750 Super Sports came with PHF 32 AD/AS carburettors with air-filters and choke attachments. They also had Conti mufflers rather than Lafranconis.

The silver-painted frame and other cycle parts also followed that of the 1978 900 Super Sport. Lights and switches were CEV rather than Aprilia, indicators were from the 900 SD, and the taillight was the larger type on the metal bracket. Instruments were Veglia and the instrument panel was as the 1978 900 Super Sport. Where the 1979 750 Super Sport deviated slightly from the specification of its larger brother was in the use of a black plastic Verlicchi throttle and the 'Goldline' Brembo 08 brake callipers that would also be fitted to the 1979 Mike Hailwood Replica. These only used one bleed nipple, and lacked the plastic brake pad cover. As the wheels were still the wire-spoked type, the rear disc was still 229mm in diameter.

These 1979 750 Super Sports were also the final bevel-gear 750s. Because they featured many of the important engine and electrical updates of the 900 SD, together with unique components such as the 'Goldline' brakes, they were particularly attractive examples. That only very few were made adds to their appeal, and 25 of the 30 went to Australia.

When the black and gold 900 Super Sport made it to the production line, it was close in specification to the blue and silver, except for the colours, wheels, rear brake and fuel taps. The frame was black, as were the air-filter boxes. Instead of the polished alloy Borrani rims laced to cast alloy hubs, the cast magnesium Speedline wheels that were being fitted to the Darmah at that time were used. The front Speedline was the same size as before, WM3 x 18 inches, but the rear increased slightly to WM4 (2.5 inches) x 18 inches. They used a four-bolt brake disc mount, but the revised rear spacing required the rear disc to increase in diameter to 280mm (11 inches). All the cast-iron discs were drilled, the rear now needing a larger alloy brake calliper support plate. Another small change that coincided with the black and gold 900 Super Sport was the Marzocchi fork leg dust seals, which were shaped differently and made of more flexible rubber.

Despite the slight increase in rear rim width, it was undoubtedly for fashion that the wheels were changed to cast magnesium, and when it came to the reality of road use they were a less than satisfactory modification. While light, the Speedlines (and the earlier Campagnolos) were prone to deterioration and corrosion. All 1979 900 Super Sports had Speedline wheels, but continual problems would soon see them replaced by an aluminium alloy FPS type. In particular, persistent breakages of Speedline wheels saw them (and the Campagnolos) being recalled and replaced

by FPS in Australia during 1981.

Despite the use of cast alloy wheels, the 1979 and 1980 black and gold 900 Super Sports had considerable allure, especially for those brought up with British bikes. The new colour scheme was very successful in creating a more modern look for what was by then an ageing design, albeit still functionally excellent. Engine specifications remained as before, with either 32mm or 40mm Dell'Orto carburettors and Lafranconi mufflers. The 40mm Dell'Ortos were without choke assemblies even though the carburettor bodies had provision for them. During 1979 the 32mm Dell'Ortos received revised jetting and designation (PHF 32 CD/CS) to keep the bike legal in the United States. The air screws were sealed, presumably so as to be tamper-proof.

All the frame and cycle parts were carried through from the final 1978 900 Super Sports. The frame was painted black, there was either a single or dual seat, CEV switches, and Veglia instruments. The Brembo brake calliers were still the early type, with machined bodies and two bleed nipples, and also used the narrow brake pads. Following the release of the Mike Hailwood Replica in the latter part of 1979 an aluminium upper fairing support was fitted across the upper triple clamp on some Super Sports. As this attached to the steering head bolt it was not possible to fit the friction steering damper that had been a feature of all the earlier Super Sports.

Production of the 900 Super Sport was 1,014 for 1979, and the engine and frame numbers moved into the 089000 series; some engines featured a 'D' stamped above the DM860. The Mike Hailwood Replica was now also in production and efforts were being put into improving the Darmah and releasing the Pantah. The Mike Hailwood Replica shared Super Sport engines (also using engine numbers from the Super Sport series), escalating the numbers

OVERLEAF *The 1980 black Super Sports received aluminium FPS wheels (with polished rims), and 'Goldline' Brembo brake calliers. The air-cleaners are non-standard.* (Geoffrey Lea)

considerably during this period. To further confuse matters, even though they shared the engine number sequence, the Mike Hailwood Replicas used a different frame number series.

In line with the changes that were occurring on the 900 SD, the Lafranconi mufflers finally departed towards the end of 1979. Their replacements, Silentiums, were undoubtedly more aesthetically pleasing, but still no Conti, which as usual were always listed as an option. With the Silentium mufflers came a change in tyre specification, from Michelin to Pirelli. On the front was now a 100/90V18 MT29 Phantom, and on the rear a 110/90V18 MT28 Phantom.

The 900 Super Sport continued into 1980 with only minor modifications, and production was reduced slightly, to 833 units. Two engine changes occurred. First, from 10 January 1980, there was the unification of crankshaft types between all the 860cc bevel-gear engines. This affected the 900 Super Sport, 900 SD and 900 SSD. The only difference between the two types were the con-rods and inner lubricating system. Kickstart models now used a crankshaft without a 2mm diameter lubricating hole on the left shaft. As all crankshafts were now unified, a closed bush needed to be fitted over the lubricating hole for the electric start bearing. All con-rods now used a dual rib around the big-end.

The second modification was to the vertical cylinder head camshafts, where a new camshaft with a reducing bush was inserted inside the lubrication hole. If the reducing bush was not fitted to these camshafts serious engine damage could result. There was also a change to the plastic alternator and ignition engine side cover plugs. The plug screwing into the covers was now metal in line with that on the contemporary 500 SL Pantah.

While there were a few detail alterations to the cycle parts, generally the black and gold Super Sport continued unchanged into 1980. The fuel taps became the grey plastic Paioli that were being standardised throughout the range. All Super Sports were now fitted with the dual seat, with a single seat still an option. Finally, the magnesium five-spoke Speedline wheels were changed to six-spoke aluminium FPSs that were not much heavier but resisted corrosion more effectively. The first FPS wheels fitted to 900 Super Sports were painted gold, but with polished aluminium rims. They generally had four bolt holes for the brake discs, but some 900 Super Sports came with the six-bolt discs with alloy carriers.

Most of the 1980 900 Super Sports also received the 'Goldline' Brembo brake callipers that had been fitted to the 1979 750 Super Sport and Mike Hailwood Replica. In line with the latter, the rear brake light pressure switch moved from the master cylinder to the brake calliper attachment.

That there were so few changes to the specification during 1980 indicated that the motorcycle was about to be revamped. The final version of the 900 Super Sport was already being developed, and was displayed at the Bologna Show in December 1980. In the meantime its status had been downgraded by the introduction of the Mike Hailwood Replica.

CHAPTER 6

Mike Hailwood Replica

While the victory at Imola in 1972 may have been the most historically significant for Ducati, Mike Hailwood's win in the TT Formula 1 race of 1978 had a stronger emotional impact for most Ducati enthusiasts around the world. After all, Mike Hailwood was a legendary figure in the world of motorcycle racing and one of the sport's rare folk heroes. To come out of retirement at the age of 38 to win again at the Isle of Man only confirmed what so many already believed, that he was possibly the greatest rider ever. And to win on a Ducati where he failed on the Yamahas vindicated his choice of mount.

The reason Hailwood chose a Ducati to race in the TT Formula 1 race went back to 1977. Then living in New Zealand, he had made a few trips to Australia to race a Manx Norton in classic events, the culmination of which was an entry in the Castrol Six Hour Production race at Amaroo Park, Sydney, in October 1977, teamed with his mate Jim Scaysbrook. Ducati, though still to win this prestigious event, had always figured prominently, but rather than race a 900 against the big boys, Hailwood's chosen mount was a Ducati 750 Super Sport. The 1977 model had a left-side gearshift, as Hailwood could no longer shift on the right, a legacy of his horrific car crash at the Nürburgring in 1974. The pair had an almost faultless race, finishing sixth overall, and first in the 750 class.

When a return to the island was mused, that Six Hour ride was fresh in his memory. Even though the Isle of Man deal included works 250, 500 and 750cc Yamahas, Hailwood wanted a Ducati for the Formula 1 event. The Ducati factory responded by sending three NCR Formula 1 bikes to Sports Motorcycles in Manchester where Steve Wynne prepared them. They were shipped very late, still residing in Bologna in April, but as soon as he got them Wynne completely stripped and reassembled the bikes, installing US Venolia Teflon-coated 11:1 pistons and Girling shocks in place of the Marzocchis. In race trim for Hailwood, the bike weighed in at only 360lb (163kg) and maximum power at the rear wheel was 80.5bhp at 8,500rpm. All three bikes were entered; Hailwood rode one, Roger Nicholls another, and Hailwood's Australian partner Jim Scaysbrook the other NCR.

As the TT regulations were quite free, certainly compared to later World Superbike events, the NCR Formula 1 bikes used light Daspa frames and engines with narrow crankcases with a spin-on oil-filter, but lacked the detail touches of the

OVERLEAF *TT Formula 1 NCR racers were a catalogued model in 1978 for those with good contacts at the factory. The bike Mike Hailwood rode at the Isle of Man that year was identical to this, except that he had his gearshift converted to the left side. The red and silver colour scheme was the official factory racing livery that year.*

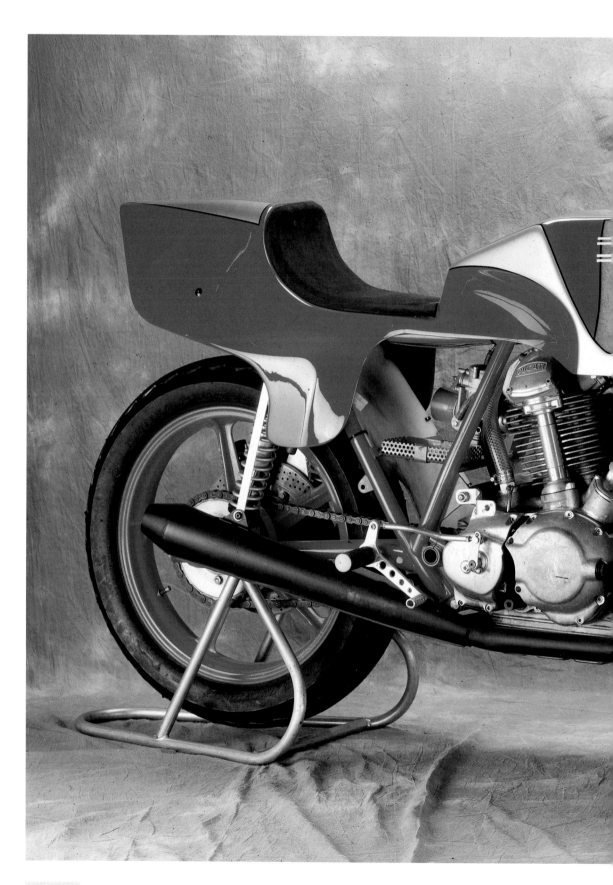

endurance bikes such as the quick-release rear wheel and beautifully machined rear disc carriers. For 1978 the engines were part 900 SS, part 750 SS: 900 heads and barrels on a round-case 750 cam geartrain. They even had the 750 ignition points, which Wynne replaced with an electronic Lucas Rita. The narrower sump allowed the use of low pipes rather than the high Imola-type, and all these engines had a dry clutch and external oil-cooler mounted in the front of the fairing. As the NCR bikes came with the gearshift on the right side (via a 750 selector box) with the brake on the left, Hailwood had a conversion with the gearshift crossover shaft going through the swing-arm pivot. The Formula 1 bikes also featured the beautifully styled one-piece fibreglass tank/fairing unit of the endurance bikes.

The six-lap TT Formula 1 race took place on 3 June 1978. Hailwood started 50 seconds behind Phil Read's works Honda, but soon caught and overtook him on the long twisting climb from Ramsey up Snaefell. After the fuel stop Read was back in front, but Hailwood's relentlessness saw the Honda expire under the pressure. All Hailwood had to do now was cruise to the finish. After more than two hours he completed the race at an average speed of 108.512mph (174.637km/h). Following a standing start lap of 109.87mph (176.92km/h), Hailwood set the fastest lap on lap two, 110.627mph (178.037km/h).

The Ducati appealed to Hailwood. 'It handles well because it is a complete machine. Everything works properly. The frame is terrific. The brakes worked well and of course the engine is all part of it. It improves the handling because it is lower and lighter. A very compact bike. On the other hand it was only 860cc against 1,000cc. So we lacked a lot of acceleration and on our dyno test we were 20 horse-power down on the others. But taken all round it was better than the other bikes.'

Again Taglioni's philosophy had been vindicated. There was also a sense of poetry in Hailwood's return. He was back on a Ducati, the bike on which he had won his first Grand Prix victory nearly 20 years earlier, in 1959.

One week after the Isle of Man Formula 1 race, on 11 June 1978, at the traditional Mallory Park post-TT event, Hailwood again won the Formula 1 race on the Ducati.

A left-side view of the same TT1 machine. The narrow crankcases allowed for low exhaust pipes, and they also featured a spin-on oil-filter. The one-piece fibreglass tank/seat unit was one of those styling miracles that occasionally emanate from Ducati.

Averaging 93.184mph (149.984km/h) with a fastest lap of 94.737mph (152.464km/h), he convincingly beat John Cowie (980 Peckett and McNab Kawasaki) and Phil Read (888 Honda). With this victory Hailwood also showed that the Ducati was at home on the traditional British short circuit.

There were two more outings that year on the Sports Motorcycles Ducati, at Donington and Silverstone. At Donington, in July, a broken piston ring caused him to ride harder than the Dunlop tyres would allow, and he crashed, but not before setting the fastest lap in the race. For Silverstone, a wider 3.5-inch Campagnolo wheel was fitted together with a front slick to replace the intermediate, giving problems with the Marzocchi suspension. With the Ducati well and truly out-gunned, this time Hailwood could only manage third.

A few months later he ended the year with another ride in the Australian Castrol Six Hour race. Unfortunately he ended up

last away (a Le Mans start was used and kickstart bikes were severely disadvantaged), but still managed to work his way through the field to lead the 750 class. The race ended for Hailwood when his co-rider Scaysbrook crashed.

As had happened after Imola, Ducati, so pleased with this success, promised street Mike Hailwood Replicas. Because the company was in the process of being absorbed by the VM Group, these were even slower in making an appearance than the first 750 Super Sport, and the 1979 TT Formula 1 race had been run before a prototype appeared. Following the 1978 success, Hailwood had agreed to ride a Ducati at the 1979 TT, both in the Formula 1 and Classic, but this time Ducati were to provide the bikes themselves rather than via the NCR umbrella. At a test session at Misano, Hailwood crashed before any improvements could be tested. The 950cc TT Classic bikes had a square-section

One of the several 1978 NCR Formula One bikes claiming to be that used by Mike Hailwood to win at the Isle of Man. Hailwood's bike had the gearshift converted to the left with a rod through the swingarm pivot. (Roy Kidney)

swing-arm, with a re-routed exhaust pipe behind the rear subframe.

Problems with management over insurance almost meant that there would be no factory bikes for Hailwood. However, at the last moment Ducati agreed to provide not only the bikes but also some of their most experienced factory mechanics, Franco Farnè, Rino Caracchi and Nani Nero. When the TT Formula 1 and Classic racers eventually arrived in May 1979 they differed considerably from the 1978 bikes, revised TT regulations ensuring that the Formula 1 bikes now used modified wet clutch square-case 860cc engines. Initial testing at Oulton Park showed both bikes to be inferior to the previous year, so Wynne replaced the swing-arm with an earlier type, and even tried the 1978 frame. The 950cc bike handled so poorly that Hailwood elected to ride a Suzuki RGB500 in the Classic. Even the Formula 1 bike was no match for that of the previous year, Hailwood's best practice lap being only 105.88mph (170.4km/h). The production-based 900 SS engine did not produce enough power, and the best he could manage was fifth. By the end of the race he was running with only four gears, a loose

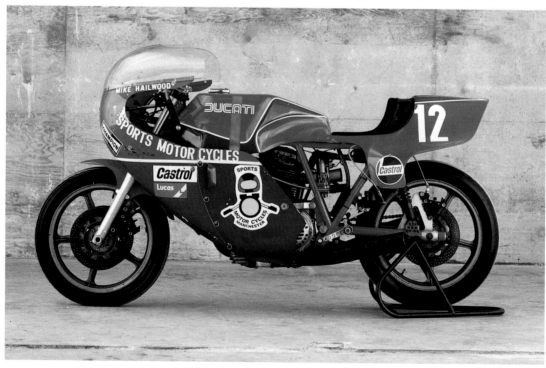

battery and a cracked exhaust pipe. It was an unfortunate follow-up to the magnificent 1978 result, and Hailwood declined to ride the F1 Ducati in the post-TT events of 1979.

Despite these disappointing results, development of a production Mike Hailwood Replica continued, and only a few months later was displayed at the London Show. Ducati took many more liberties with the term 'replica' on this bike than they had with the 1974 Super Sport. The factory documentation relating to the Mike Hailwood Replica in 1979 was almost apologetic for the unremarkable specification. 'It does not represent a new design since, even if the factory made a true reproduction of the TT machine, the strict and rigorous race regulations imposed by the English authorities for this class must be followed.' Thus the Mike Hailwood Replica was purely a cosmetic alteration of a 900 Super Sport and initially carried the title 900 SS MHR.

Like the black and gold 900 Super Sport of only a few months earlier, when the Mike Hailwood Replica was first released it was primarily aimed at the UK market. The 1979 show bike featured a one-piece fairing with large 'Mike Hailwood Replica' lettering, and a fibreglass cover over the steel Super Sport fuel tank. Originally it was intended to market the Replica with a fibreglass tank with an 'Imola' and NCR-style clear strip for fuel level reading. A prototype with a fibreglass tank was constructed and used on some publicity brochures, but as the bike was built primarily for the UK market the tank was changed for both the show and production versions. The dual seat came with a removable cover, and there were the Nippon Denso instruments and switch gear from the Darmah. It also featured Darmah magnesium Speedline wheels with four-bolt drilled front disc brake rotors. The frame was red and styling followed the lines of the NCR racers, without bodywork side covers. Colours of red, white and green were the same Castrol colours as Hailwood's Formula 1 bikes, usual NCR colours being red and silver.

The first Mike Hailwood Replica of 1979 had a one-piece fairing and no side covers. This factory prototype has a fibreglass fuel tank and FPS wheels, while production bikes used a fibreglass cover over a steel Super Sport tank, and Speedline wheels.

When they appeared, the first Mike Hailwood Replicas of 1979 were very similar to the London show bike.

There were 200 of the first series of Mike Hailwood Replicas, and most were sold in Britain. They were also available in other countries, but in fewer numbers, and all 200 came with a certificate. The engine was identical to the 1979 900 Super Sport, but these first 200 came with Dell'Orto PHM 40 AD/AS carburettors and Conti mufflers. Even though the Dell'Orto bodies had provision for choke attachments, they came only with tickler buttons. Engine numbers continued with the DM860 089000 series of the 1979 black-and-gold 900 Super Sports; as the engines for both were identical they shared the same number sequence. All the alterations that were made to the entire 860 engine range appeared on the Hailwood Replica, which meant that it received the later uniform crankshaft. There were also changes to the gear selector plunger at the rear of the crankcase, countershaft nut and seals, and alternator rotor and stator. In addition there were reshaped exhaust header pipes, the left-side exhaust in particular now being much closer into the engine to aid the shape of the fairing; this made for more difficult oil level checking but significantly improved ground clearance. For the first time two sets of oversize valves were officially listed as an option: 42mm inlet and 38mm exhaust valves, and 44mm inlet and 40mm exhaust valves.

What set the Mike Hailwood Replica apart from the 900 Super Sport were a number of changes to the cycle parts. While still using the DM 860 SS designation, the red-painted frame of the Replica started with the same number sequence of the earlier 900 SD, 900001. This meant that the frame numbers of the 1979 Replicas were the same as the 1977 Darmahs, even though the frames were quite different. To avoid confusion, the Darmah received new frame number designations as soon as the Mike Hailwood Replica went into production.

The Hailwood Replica frame came in for a few small alterations from the Super Sport, noticeably the absence of side cover retaining lugs. A longer centrestand was also fitted to allow for longer shock absorbers, but it was with the bodywork that there were the most changes from the regular Super Sport.

Patterned on Hailwood's 1979 Formula 1 Ducati rather than the more successful 1978 bike, a one-piece fibreglass racing-style fairing was fitted. Front turn signal indicators were flush-mounted on the fairing, with a plastic gasket as usual sealing the headlamp. Unlike the Super Sport, the fairing had an aluminium upper cross-brace that was attached by a circlip to the steering head retaining nut. This meant that the usual friction steering damper was not able to be fitted. Removal and installation of the fairing was a time-consuming operation and required tasks such as oil level checking even for basic maintenance, which did not make the Mike Hailwood Replica the most practical of motorcycles.

Evidence that the Hailwood Replica was hastily conceived was indicated by the use of an 18-litre 900 Super Sport steel fuel tank underneath a fibreglass cover. Purely to appease British regulations, which banned fibreglass fuel tanks, this tank cover also had a shape similar to that of the NCR racers. While the design of the fuel tank graphics was the same as later Hailwood Replicas, the distinguishing feature of the 1979 Replica was the location of the white 'DUCATI' decals on the fibreglass tank cover. As with the pre-production 750 Super Sport of 1973, these were mounted very high on both sides, almost to the top of the cover.

The seat unit also mirrored the shape of the NCR racers, with no side covers and the battery and regulator clearly visible on the right, and the 40mm Dell'Orto carburettor on the left. The fibreglass seat and tail unit was unique to this model, with the solo seat attached to a fibreglass rear cover supplied as standard. A dual seat was an option. Both these seat pads were particularly crudely constructed, almost looking aftermarket rather than factory supplied.

The red mudguards were similar in shape to those on the 900 Super Sport, and the large taillight, rear indicators and 55/60-watt halogen headlamp, all CEV, were identical. Other

All 1979 Mike Hailwood Replicas came with unfiltered 40mm Dell'Orto carburettors and Conti mufflers. The seat padding looked aftermarket and a new pad needed to be inserted to make it a dual seat.

electrical equipment, fusebox, ignition, relays and horn, was shared with the 900 SSD Darmah. The instruments and switch gear were also SSD rather than the Super Sport. Nippon Denso instruments, a 140mph speedometer on the left and 8,000rpm-redlined tachometer on the right, were used, but those for other European markets had a kilometres-per-hour speedometer. The warning light console was as for the Darmah. Because the console did not need to clamp the handlebars to the top triple clamp, this was from the 900 SSD. Even though no sidestand was fitted, there was still a red stand warning light on the dashboard.

The left-side switch block was also Nippon Denso from the 900 SD and SSD, and the usual 1979 Super Sport black plastic Verlicchi twin-cable throttle without any wiring used. There was no electric start or engine kill switch on the Hailwood Replica. Handgrips were Super Sport Verlicchi, and the clip-on handlebars had a different mounting angle to clear the wider fuel tank. As with the Super Sport, the clutch and brake levers were black, with a new type of clutch adjuster. All the alloy foot levers and folding steel footpegs were from the 1978–79 Super Sport.

While the Brembo master cylinders were Super Sport specification, the Hailwood Replica received the racing-style Brembo 'Goldline' 08 brake callipers front and rear that had first appeared on the 1979 750

Mike Hailwood Replicas shared their Nippon Denso instruments and switches with the Darmah.

and 900 Super Sports. Unlike the earlier Super Sport type these had only one bleed screw, but were also without plastic pad covers. The front 280mm cast-iron discs were drilled, with a four-bolt wheel attachment. The cast alloy wheels used a rear disc identical to those on the front, with a correspondingly larger alloy brake calliper bracket. Another change from the specification of the Super Sport was the rear brake light pressure switch, which moved from the master cylinder to the brake calliper (although the Super Sport soon followed suit).

In line with the 1979 900 Super Sport, gold-painted Speedline cast magnesium wheels graced most of the 1979 Mike Hailwood Replicas, being the usual fitment to Darmahs and Super Sports at that time; however, some bikes were fitted with the gold Campagnolos that had featured on the 1977 900 SD. Both sets of wheels had the same rim size, 2.15 x 18 front and 2.50 x 18 rear, and all Hailwood Replicas were shod with Pirelli Phantom tyres, MT29 100/90V18 on the front and MT28 110/90V18 on the rear.

Functionally the Marzocchi forks, with 38 x 580mm fork tubes, were identical to those of the Super Sport, differing only in that the fork legs were polished aluminium. As with other V-twins the triple clamps were painted black. In an effort to improve the already marginal ground clearance of the Super Sport and prevent the fairing from grounding, longer Marzocchi shock absorbers were fitted. At 330mm (13 inches) these were 20mm longer than the 900 Super Sport, leading to a tall 800mm (31^1/2-inch) seat height.

After the first 200 Mike Hailwood Replicas of September 1979, there were a few small modifications to the next series of 100 bikes built towards the end of that year,

The 1979 and 1980 Replicas featured Brembo 'Goldline' brake callipers. This publicity bike has gold FPS wheels.

By 1980 the seat had been revised and steel fuel tanks were fitted to the Mike Hailwood Replica. The battery and regulator were still exposed.

with a further 447 during 1980. A 24-litre steel fuel tank replaced the earlier Super Sport example with its crude fibreglass cover. The fuel filler cap on this tank opened towards the rider as it had on the earlier Imola-style tanks, and the positioning of the white 'DUCATI' decals was lower, but not always straight. There was also a new fibreglass seat base with a better-finished dual seat. This was now easily transformed into a single seat with the addition of a fibreglass cover that included a rear pad. The decals on the seat cover were the same as before.

The one-piece fairing was retained, but all bikes now had the small 'Mike Hailwood Replica' decals. At some stage during 1980 the fairing also received large white 'DUCATI' decals. As with the first model, there were no side covers for 1980, the battery, regulator and rear carburettor remaining clearly visible.

Many of the next series of Hailwood Replicas (after the first 200) had five-spoke magnesium Campagnolo wheels before these, too, were replaced with six-spoke aluminium FPSs. Unlike the 900 Super Sport, the Hailwood Replica did not receive the FPS wheels with a four-bolt disc attachment, all being six-bolt, with the 280mm drilled discs with alloy carriers. Like the contemporary Darmah and Super Sport, early FPS wheels had gold spokes but polished aluminium rims. During 1980 the fork legs were also painted black, keeping the bike more in line with the Super Sport.

Mike Hailwood died tragically in a motor car accident on 22 March 1981. Despite defying death on the Isle of Man where he won 14 TT events, he died in a motorway crash as he returned home from a fish and chip shop with his two children. Shortly before his death Ducati had already announced a revised version of the Mike Hailwood Replica and, despite the tragedy, decided to continue with its production. It would remain the flagship of the range until the demise of the bevel-gear engine.

CHAPTER 7

The end of the line

By 1980 it seemed to many that the Ducati Super Sport was past its 'use-by' date. Now into its eighth year essentially unchanged, and without a major international race win to its credit in 1979, the design was perhaps starting to show its age. However, again it was Montjuich Park that proved that there was still some life left in the venerable Super Sport.

On 5–6 July 1980 José Mallol and Alejandro Tejedo rode their locally prepared 900 Super Sport in the annual Barcelona 24 Hour race, the fourth round of the Endurance World Championship. Entering only because it was the final round of Spain's national endurance championship, Mallol and Tejedo ended up leading the final seven hours after all the favourites either crashed or broke down. At an average speed of 119.28km/h (74.12mph) they completed two more laps than the second-placed Honda. The bike being essentially a modified 864cc square-case Super Sport, this was an exceptional victory against specialised racing machinery.

Things were also changing at the factory. During 1978 Ducati Meccanica had become part of Finmeccanica in the VM Group of government-controlled companies. This meant a change of emphasis that not only affected production, but eventually also quality. Fortunately the Barcelona victory showed that the 900 Super Sport was worth preserving and a revised version was developed for 1981.

The Mike Hailwood Replica assumed the status of range leader and the 900 Super Sport was downgraded to a supporting role. Fundamentally unchanged from earlier examples, it received a moderate facelift that would see it through until its demise a year later. The biggest changes were to the styling of the dual seat, together with a new colour scheme of silver with stripes in three shades of blue. The fairing was now silver rather than blue, and also featured the same stripes.

The period from 1981 until 1983 was a period of instability at Bologna, and there was inconsistency in the specification of many of these final Super Sports that harked back to the 750s of 1974. However, the reasons for these inconsistencies were now different from those of the mid-1970s. Much of the Borgo Panigale plant was being used to build diesel engines for the VM Group. Gradually, as VM's interest in diesel engines increased, the management of the motorcycle division came under increasing pressure to become more profitable. Morale was low and quality control not particularly good during this period. Engine assembly was haphazard, and while the design was improved, the quality of many of the engine components was not up to the standard of the earlier bikes.

Buoyed by the addition of the Mike Hailwood Replicas using the same engine number sequence, the Super Sport engine numbers had by now reached the 090000 series. Some engines had a 'D' stamped above the DM860, but this was not significant. During 1981 several engine improvements began to filter through the entire bevel-twin line-up, many being the most important since the Darmah modification of 1977. Production also increased to 1,205 for the year.

The first engine and ignition improvements occurred in early 1981. From engine number 090915 new ignition pick-ups and transducer terminal blocks were fitted, taken from the 500 SL Pantah. Later, from engine number 092220, the ignition pick-up mounting was altered to allow for the adjustment of individual air gaps, requiring modifications within the clutch cover. The four-step ignition advance curve was also altered slightly, from 6° at 900rpm, increasing to 16–18° at 1,800rpm and 28° at 2,800rpm, to the maximum advance of 32° at 4,000rpm. There was yet another alternator modification, with the rotor from the 500 SL Pantah and a return to the 860 stator; the Super Sport alternator now differed from that fitted to electric-start versions.

Also during the early part of 1981 there were revisions to the valve guides and valve guide sealing for the first time since the 750 Super Sport of 1974. All previous desmodromic engines had used only a single inner O-ring to seal the valve stem and guide, but from engine number 091022 the ring was replaced by a regular seal. It was still possible to fit guides using both sealing systems, and to modify the closing rockers of earlier engines to accept the revised system. After engine number 091267 the steel inner clutch drum, which had served the engine

In 1981 there were new colours and a revised dual seat; the single seat was no longer an option. Either 32mm or 40mm Dell'Orto carburettors were fitted, but always Silentium mufflers.

from the 860 GT, was replaced together with new clutch springs.

Another significant engine alteration occurred towards the end of 1981, from engine number 092920. The six-dog gearbox that had been used on all bevel-twins since the first 750s was replaced by a three-dog type. Racing Ducati V-twins had used three-dog gearboxes since 1977, so it was inevitable that this modification would eventually filter through to the production bikes. This modification affected all 900 engines, not just the Super Sport. With the new gearbox came primary gears in matched sets, rather than as individual gears.

Even though Dell'Orto PHF 32CD and CS carburettors were specified, most 1981 900 Super Sports came with PHM 40A model. These were without air-filters, and

Carried over from 1980 were the CEV headlight and indicators. Despite the new graphics, the look was undeniably Super Sport.

all Super Sports now came with Silentium mufflers. No longer with carburettor tickler buttons, the 40mm Dell'Ortos had chokes, the white plastic choke lever being mounted in the usual position on the left at the rear of the fuel tank. This was unlike the contemporary Hailwood Replica, which mounted the choke lever next to the headlight.

The frames were all painted black for the 1981 Super Sports, and they continued to use the earlier 900 Super Sport number sequence, which by 1981 had moved into the 089000 and 090000 series. While the 18-litre steel fuel tank was unchanged, the cap was now lockable with a separate key. For some reason earlier fuel tanks (with the older decals) also appeared on some bikes. Although the side-cover decals were the same as before, tank decals were new, and there was no longer a 'DESMO' decal on the fairing. Most 1981 Super Sports were also without the 'Made in Italy' decal on the fuel tank. The dual seat was completely new, with a removable seat pad, the base being bolted to the frame. This seat pad was fastened to the base by a lock at the rear, making a total of four separate keys: ignition, tank, seat and steering lock.

There were no alterations to the internals of the black-painted 38mm Marzocchi forks, but the top triple clamps had the 'M' Marzocchi symbol cast into them. These had revised threaded spring-retaining plugs in the top of the fork tubes that required a 30mm hexagon spanner for removal instead of the earlier 12mm Allen wrench. Still fitted at the rear were 310mm (12.2-inch) Marzocchi shock absorbers with black springs.

The six-spoke aluminium FPS wheels were now painted gold all over and took a six-bolt disc instead of the earlier four-bolt. Shared with the Hailwood Replica and 900 SSD, these six-bolt 280mm drilled cast-iron discs had detachable black alloy carriers. Until June 1981, and frame number 090602, all the 1981 900 Super Sports received 'Goldline' Brembo brake callipers, and subsequently these were unified throughout the range. There was only one bleed nipple and they had a plastic brake pad cover. For 1981 there was also a return to Michelin M45 tyres.

Handlebar switches were altered to keep the Super Sport in line with the Mike Hailwood Replica and Darmah. The left-side switch block was Nippon Denso rather than CEV, and the throttle assembly was Verlicchi black plastic. In all other respects the 1981 Super Sport was the same as the 1980: the same instrument panel with Veglia instruments, later CEV headlight and taillight, CEV 900 SD indicators, black levers, and Verlicchi handgrips.

At the same time the Mike Hailwood Replica came in for a redesign, and typically the ethos of the bike was softened slightly. While some of the changes were welcome from a practical standpoint, the Replica was no longer fitted with Conti mufflers as standard equipment. The restyling of the seat and side covers also detracted from the race replica status of the earlier bikes. The Mike Hailwood Replica again spearheaded the Super Sport line-up during 1981, with 1,500 constructed. In 1982 even more were made, 1,549, considerably more than the 900 Super Sport of that year.

The engine number sequence continued as before, and was still shared with the 900 Super Sport, some also having a 'D' stamped on the right crankcase; these started at around DM860 090800 for the first revised 900 Mike Hailwood Replicas of early 1981. As the engine number sequence was shared with the 900 Super Sport, all the engine modifications that occurred on that model during 1981 also appeared on the Hailwood Replica. While the Dell'Orto PHM 40 carburettors were still fitted, these now came with chokes and the BD and BS designation, with jetting altered slightly to meet emission requirements, and the white plastic choke lever attached to the steering head fairing bracket. During 1982 900 Super Sport air-cleaners were fitted to some Hailwood Replicas, but most had unfiltered bell mouths. Following racing practice that had found a benefit with a shorter inlet throat, there was a new type of bell mouth. Initially these were short plastic, attached by a hose clamp, but were soon replaced by an

aluminium screw-on type of similar length. There was no provision for recycled crankcase gases on those Mike Hailwood Replicas with carburettor bell mouths; a tube connected with a flapper valve was either attached to the top frame tube or the front air filter.

Even though the engine numbers continued unchanged, there was a new frame number sequence for the revised Hailwood Replica. No longer with the DM 860 SS designation, the red-painted frame now used numbers starting at DM 900 R 900001. The frame also now had a folding lifting lever on the left side, just under the bodywork, to aid with mounting the motorcycle on the centrestand, which was also fitted with two return springs. Earlier

The cockpit of the 1981 Super Sport. Unlike the Mike Hailwood Replica, Veglia instruments were still used in a plastic panel identical to that used from 1978. Switches were now Nippon Denso and the fuel tank cap was lockable.

stands were known for repeatedly banging against the frame on bumpy roads.

While the steel fuel tank and fibreglass seat base were carried over from 1980, there were new side covers; these were an unusual shape, and featured the same 'Mike Hailwood Replica' decals that appeared on the front upper fairing. As the Pantah moved towards more ABS bodywork, these side covers too were ABS, although the seat base and fairing were still fibreglass. Following on from the 900 Super Sport, the fuel cap was now lockable. Finally, after many years of Italian horns, this became a Bosch.

By far the biggest change was with the design of the fairing. Now in two parts, the upper fairing still featured the flush-mounted front indicators. All 1981 two-piece fairings had the small 'Mike Hailwood Replica' decals on the upper part, and the large white 'DUCATI' decals on the sides, underneath the white stripe. The ABS front mudguard was similar to previous designs, but by 1982 had become the squarer type as fitted to the Pantah and 900 S2, except that it was painted red. For 1981 the Marzocchi forks still had black-painted fork legs, now featuring the revised shape of the mounting for the front mudguard, and the new top triple clamps with the 'M' insignia. There were new Marzocchi forks again for 1982, sharing internals with those of the 900 S2 that appeared later that year. They had slightly longer fork tubes at 590mm, and used a shorter 221mm hydraulic damper rod, 130mm instead of 140mm, giving less fork travel. The brake callipers were still mounted in front of the fork legs.

The 1981 Replica still used 330mm (13-inch) Marzocchi shock absorbers, but for 1982 these were changed to complement the revised forks. They now offered less travel at 80mm (3.15 inches) compared with the earlier shocks' 90mm (3.5 inches).

For 1981 the Mike Hailwood Replica became the range spearhead, and many more were produced than in previous years. The fairing was now in two parts and there were side covers to hide the battery and rear carburettor.

It was yet another effort to improve the ground clearance, but this continued to be a problem. Initially the chainguard was the stainless steel item, but by 1982 this had become a red-painted steel type.

There was complete standardisation of the wheels and brake discs for 1981. The gold-painted six-spoke FPS aluminium wheels took the six-bolt 280mm drilled cast-iron discs with black alloy disc carriers,

fitted front and rear. After frame number 900504 the FPS wheels had two 8mm dowels fitted between the wheel and cush drive to prevent loosening of the assembly, always a problem on Speedline and Campagnolo wheels. The first 1981 Mike Hailwood Replicas had the Brembo 'Goldline' racing callipers of the previous model, but after frame number 901301 these were replaced by the regular black type now being standardised. Tyres were once again Michelin M45s front and rear, in sizes of 3.50V18 and 4.25/85V18.

Despite a restyled 900 Mike Hailwood Replica being displayed at the Bologna Show at the end of 1981, the production version continued into 1982 largely unchanged. This was probably fortunate because the show bike was unusually styled. The fairing had three long white stripes,

and the Silentium mufflers and FPS wheels were painted black.

For the Super Sport's final production year there were only minor alterations to the specification. The colours and styling were the same, and most Super Sports came with side covers constructed of ABS without the plastic mesh. Because of small inconsistencies in the specification of these final bikes they were obviously considered the end of the line.

While most of the significant engine alterations had occurred during 1981, improvements to the bevel-gear engine continued to appear. However, only one more update made it to the Super Sport before it was superseded by the 900 S2. From engine number 094150 the bronze valve seats were replaced with cast-iron versions. In line with the 1982 Mike Hailwood Replica, there were new, shorter aluminium bell mouths for the 40mm Dell'Orto carburettors, most Super Sports not having air-cleaners.

Only 335 900 Super Sports were built in 1982. While the Mike Hailwood Replica, together with the kickstart 900 S2, continued into and beyond the 095000 engine series, the end was in sight for the kickstart engine. In 1983, in the late 096000 series, production ended. Between 1975 and 1984 a total of 10,924 kickstart engines had been produced, the final 985 being used in the non-Super Sport models, the MHR and S2.

During 1982 some Super Sports were fitted with black-painted Mike Hailwood Replica frames that featured a folding lever on the rear left subframe to help when putting the bike on the centrestand. There were also some further changes to the bodywork. Following the example of the Pantah and 900 S2, the larger and more angular front mudguard was fitted to some Super Sports (still silver), with both the front and rear mudguards still constructed of fibreglass. While most bikes had the ABS side

The right-side view of the same restored 1981 900 Mike Hailwood Replica. While hardly a limited production machine, it was a very desirable motorcycle. For 1982 it remained largely unchanged.

covers, it was typical of the inconsistency of production at this time that some Super Sports also came with the earlier type. All fairings featured an upper aluminium cross-brace and there was a return to the 'Desmo' decal on the lower sides of the fairing. The 1982 Super Sport no longer had the chromed *Belli* horn, but the black Bosch from the Darmah.

The final alteration was to the front

forks, which were now sharing internals with the Marzocchi forks of the 1982 Mike Hailwood Replica and 900 S2. Another inconsistency was that on some Super Sports the chainguard was now black, the same as the 750 Sport, rather than stainless steel.

Production of the 900 Super Sport ceased during 1982 at around engine number 095000. The frame numbers had reached the 091000 series, which would be continued by the Super Sport replacement, the 900 S2. By now the Super Sport was becoming difficult to sell, and many were sold at discount prices in some markets, particularly Australia. With total production of 6,323 over eight years, the 900 Super Sport had earned the status of the 'classic' bevel-gear Ducati. Right until the end it used as many Italian components as

Two 1982 900 Super Sports. Looking closely at these two bikes gives an indication of the inconsistencies of production during this period. One has a 1978 fuel tank, the other a 1978 front mudguard.

possible; even with Bosch ignition and Nippon Denso switches, Ducati resisted fitting it with Nippon Denso instruments. Eventually a kickstart 900cc twin with early 1970s suspension was an anachronism in a world wanting increased sophistication. While the Mike Hailwood Replica came in for a major redesign and was saved, the Super Sport disappeared, although it would be revived seven years later.

CHAPTER 8

Not quite a Super Sport

As the 900 Super Sport was being transformed into the Mike Hailwood Replica, plans were simultaneously under way to expand the Super Sport concept in another direction, that of the sport touring 900 SD Darmah, to produce a softer version with electric start and no solo seat option. The result was the 900 Super Sport Desmo Darmah, or SSD. It was an attractive bike, but flawed in its conception. To the real enthusiast a Super Sport was always a minimalist motorcycle, a sport bike with no excess flab, and at 216kg (436lb) the SSD was hardly that. It was a Super Sport with middle age spread.

Taking an essentially 900 SD engine, frame and running gear, and clothing it with a Super Sport-style half fairing and café racer riding position, the 900 SSD was first unveiled at the Bologna show in November 1978. Surprisingly, the bike made it into production almost immediately.

The electric-start engine was identical to the 900 SD, and shared the same engine number sequence. Engine numbers began after DM860 903762, so all SSDs came without a kickstart. Even though 900 SSD Darmah engines used the revised cylinder heads with the 58mm wide inlet studs that enabled 40mm carburettor manifolds to bolt on, carburettors were Dell'Orto PHF 32 AD/AS with twin air-filters. These were complemented by the usual ugly Lafranconi mufflers. By April 1979 the carburation had changed to Dell'Orto PHF 32 CD/CS carbu-

rettors with slightly revised jetting, and Silentium mufflers.

While the frame and running gear were essentially 900 SD, the 900 SSD used a different frame number designation, all beginning with DM 900 SD. To confuse matters, the number sequence was shared with the 900 SD, and started from 902960. All 900 SSD Darmahs had the longer SD 275mm centrestand, and unlike the 900 Super Sport had a sidestand fitted.

In late 1979, so as not to be confused with the Mike Hailwood Replica, the 900 SD also started to use frames with a DM 900 SD designation, and a new number sequence beginning at 950001. Thus from September of that year the 900 SD and 900 SSD shared frame numbers, although the SSD frame had additional brackets for footpeg location.

Most of the cycle parts were also 900 SD. The 15-litre fuel tank, duck-tail seat and removable seat pad came from the first-series Darmah, but with a two-tone blue colour scheme. Decals were new for the 900 SSD and a fibreglass half fairing was fitted, while 900 SD stainless steel mudguards were used.

The instrument panel and fairing were located in Super Sport fashion on a bracket from the steering head. All the Nippon Denso instruments and warning lights, throttle, levers, handgrips, switch gear, Bosch 180mm 55/60 halogen headlight, and large CEV taillight and CEV turn signal indicators were shared with the 900 SD Darmah. Also like the 900 SD, a seven-position Paioli steering connected the right fork leg to the frame front downtube.

Where the 900 SSD differed from the SD was in the plastic instrument warning light holder on the instrument panel, which bolted to the steering head bracket; as it did not need to clamp the handlebars to the upper fork yoke it was the same as that fitted to the Mike Hailwood Replica. There were new clip-on handlebars for the SSD, quite unlike those of the regular 900 Super Sport. These mounted on the fork legs and featured a forward offset like the last 750 Sport handlebars, but were also raised, placing the bars at the height of the top triple clamp. To complement the forward handlebars, rear-set foot controls were provided. A small bracket was welded on the frame so the pegs were positioned at the bottom of the side cover. Folding metal footpegs were fitted, with a 1978 Super Sport aluminium gear lever. The levers provided a very high, and rearward, footpeg position that would be changed the following year. Because the 900 SSD had rear-set controls, the passenger footrests were also rear-set via two metal pegs that bolted to the muffler mount.

All 900 SSDs came with 38mm Marzocchi forks with polished aluminium fork legs. Fork tubes were 38 x 600 mm, and the fork triple clamps were painted black. The 330mm (13-inch) shock absorbers were oleo-pneumatic Marzocchi. For 1979 SSDs had cast magnesium Speedline wheels, but these differed from those on the 900 SD and Super Sport by having a six-bolt mount for the brake discs. The three 280mm discs were drilled, and had aluminium carriers. The Brembo brake callipers and master cylinders were 900 SD, rather than 900 SS, specification, and the tyres were also the same as the 900 SD of 1979, Pirelli Gordon 3.50H18 and 120/90V18.

The 900 SSD used the duck-tail seat of the 1977–78 900 SD Darmah, and all the running gear was shared with the Darmah rather than the Super Sport. This 1980 model has the later footpegs and controls.

Polished Marzocchi forks featured on all 900 SSDs, as did the front brake discs with six-bolt attachments. The fairing, while similar to that of the Super Sport, was shaped differently.

The 900 SSD continued in production on a limited scale during 1980, still sharing engines with the 900 SD; thus all the alterations to the engine of the latter also affected the SSD. These were the unification of crankshafts between the Super Sport and Darmah, alterations to the vertical cylinder head camshaft, and (after engine number 904414) a shorter gearshift selector shaft and new clutch side cover. This required a revised gearshift arrangement. Production of the 900 SSD had finished by the end of 1980, around engine number 905900, so the final machines received some of the changes that were made in late 1980 and early 1981. These included new ignition pick-ups and transducers, clutch drum, valve guides and valve guide seals.

In line with the 900 SD and 900 Super Sport, the Speedline wheels became aluminium FPS, still with six-bolt discs. Initially these had a polished aluminium rim, but were later all gold. The biggest change was to the footpegs, gearshift and brake lever, which occurred after frame number 950762, coinciding with engine number 904414 when a shorter (134mm) selector shaft was fitted. A new clutch cover allowed the gearshift lever to be lower and further forward without touching the engine cover. Although the frame still had the earlier footpeg mounting points, the footpegs were now mounted on brackets that bolted to the frame below the swing-arm pivot. This resulted in rear set footpegs lower and further forward than before, and required different pegs, brake and gearshift levers, and control rods. The passenger footpegs no longer required the extra bracket and were mounted in their usual place as the muffler fasteners.

Regular production of the 900 Super Sport Desmo Darmah finished around frame number 952100; because it shared all its engine and frame numbers with the SD, it is very difficult to determine the exact numbers produced, and the factory production data group the two together. Of the 2,251 Darmahs built in 1979 and 1980, the 900 SSD would probably have accounted for about a quarter. As with some other 900 Ducatis of this period, 900 SSDs continued to be built sporadically in small numbers as late as 1983 and 1984, but these were probably left-overs from earlier production.

By now the 1981 line-up had been formalised and the 900 SSD was not to play a part, Ducati deciding to concentrate on expanding production of the more successful Mike Hailwood Replica. Thus the bevel-twins became standardised into two

versions, kickstart and electric start, the latter engines now only fitted to the 900 SD. Kickstart motors remained for the 900 Super Sport and Mike Hailwood Replica, but by 1982 it was clear that their days were numbered. Kickstart-only engines were now an anachronism.

The factory response was to create another Darmah and Super Sport hybrid,

While the tank was the same as the 900 SD, the different colour scheme was striking, making the 900 SSD one of Ducati's more attractive models. All SSDs were electric start only.

similar in concept to the ill-fated 900 SSD. The result was the 900 S2, a motorcycle that somehow failed to combine any of the strengths of either of its ancestors. As an electric-start sports tourer the Darmah was superior, and as a full sporting bike the S2 was only a pale imitation of a real Super Sport. The 900 S2 made its appearance about the middle of 1982, in two versions, kick and electric start. Many more were built with electric start (476 compared with 173 kickstart in 1982), but the 900 S2 soon replaced both the electric start 900 SD and kickstart 900 Super Sport.

Whereas the 900 SSD was merely a cosmetic alteration of a 900 SD, the 900 S2 was the first redesign of the concept since the 900 SD Darmah of 1977. There were few major engine changes, but what was changed was the rationale of the motorcycle. Unfortunately it was also a motorcycle without a clear identity. When it was first released it used the engines of both the Super Sport and Darmah; the kickstart engines continued with the Super Sport engine number series, from around DM860 095700, while the electric-start engine numbers were the same as the 900 SD, and began around DM860 907000.

Several alterations to the engine specification occurred early in the life of the 900 S2. From engine number 095742 (kickstart) and 907429 (electric start) a new gearshift drum was fitted. Another alternator and regulator modification appeared at the end of 1982, after engine number 096142 (kickstart) and 907232 (electric start). From 1981 different alternators had been fitted to the two engine types, and the 900 S2 continued this route.

In the cylinder head the bronze valve guides became cast-iron during 1983, being now the same for both inlet and exhaust. The cast-iron guides were still the same design as the modified type of 1981 and used the valve guide seal that fitted over the top of the guide. All S2 engines had the 75 rubber blocks between the cylinder head fins to minimise engine noise. Ignition was still the Bosch BTZ, with the final updates to the ignition pick-ups that had been made during 1981. Carburation was either by

Dell'Orto PHF 32 AD/AS or Dell'Orto PHM 40 BD/BS carburettors, though most S2s came with the latter. Unlike the 900 Super Sport, both inlet manifolds were identical, the 32mm type using a rubber O-ring as a seal. The Dell'Orto 32 AD/AS carburettors had identical jetting to those fitted on the 1974–79 860s and 900s, rather than the later leaner 32 CD/CS type. Both 32mm and 40mm carburettors came with external chokes, operated by the usual lever mounted to the left of the headlight.

A completely new exhaust system graced the 900 S2. The left exhaust header was now angled closer to the engine, as had been the case on the Mike Hailwood Replica since 1979. Either Conti or Silentium mufflers were fitted, but had their brackets mounted further back so as to fit the longer S2 frame. This all-new frame reverted back to the DM 860 SS designation and continued with the number series of the 900 Super Sport, taking over where the Super Sport left off, at around 091500. Black-painted for 1982, the straight front downtubes were flattened at the engine mounts as the 860 and 900 SD frames had been. The rear frame downtubes were bowed and internally relieved to allow for the installation of the larger Yuasa 19 Ah battery. Kickstart bikes still used the 12 Ah battery of the Super Sport, but not the earlier Super Sport frame. Because these rear frame tubes were bent and hollow, the S2 frame was not as strong as that of the earlier Super Sport. However, as the overall dimensions were larger, and the engine placed higher, this frame would form the basis of the last Mike Hailwood Replicas and S2s. The trade-off for more ground clearance was a physically larger motorcycle with a higher seat, and one that did not handle as well.

No sidestand was fitted to the 900 S2, so to help with placing the bike on the centre-stand a folding lever was placed on the left side next to the side cover, as with the 1982 Mike Hailwood Replica and some 900 Super Sports. As this was a Super Sport-derived frame the swing-arm featured the usual Seeley type of chain adjustment.

There was also completely new body-

work for the 900 S2. While the steel fuel tank was Super Sport-derived, the S2 received a new fairing and seat unit. The black lockable fuel tank cap was completely different from the type that had been fitted to every previous bevel-twin Ducati; flush mounted, and shared with the 650 SL Pantah, these caps were notorious for allowing water to enter the tank. The earlier tank caps may have had the occasional venting problem, but they were superior to the S2 type, which seemed to be more of a styling, rather than practical, alteration.

Continuing the theme of the final 900 Super Sport, the S2's fibreglass seat unit extended over the taillight around the top of the shock absorbers. Instead of a Super Sport fairing, a modified ABS 600 SL Pantah fairing was used; this was also painted grey and carried a continuation of the yellow, orange and red stripes of the seat and side covers. The 900 S2 fairing differed between the kick and electric-start versions as a cutaway was needed to clear the electric starter assembly on the left side. As with the contemporary Mike Hailwood

The 900 S2 replaced the 900 SS during 1982. The engines were shared with the SS and Darmah, but the S2 had a completely new frame and running gear. This is the first electric-start version.

Replica and Pantah, the front turn signal indicators were flush mounted in the fairing.

All the mudguards were new for the 900 S2. Up front was a black guard similar to that of the final 900 Super Sport and 600 Pantah, while the rear metal mudguard was also black, with a plastic front section. The taillight and rear indicators were also new; much larger and more angular than before, these CEV units would also feature on the next series of Mike Hailwood Replicas.

Strangely, the 900 S2, while inheriting many of the features of the Darmah, still retained its links to the Super Sport by using the 170mm CEV 55/60-watt H4 headlight. However, the instrument panel with warning lights (including the non-connected side-stand) and Nippon Denso instruments was carried over from the 900 SSD. A similar riding position to that earlier bike was provided by new clip-on handlebars. The left switch block was the usual Nippon Denso, but now a much more satisfactory Verlicchi twin-cable throttle incorporated the electric start and engine kill switch. Like many of the new parts on the S2 this came from the Pantah.

For the first time since the 750 GT and Sport of 1974, the 900 S2 featured Marzocchi forks with rear-mounted brake callipers. The forks were similar to those of the 1982 900 Mike Hailwood Replica with 38 x 590mm fork tubes and a 221mm damper rod. There was also new Marzocchi suspension at the rear. The 900 S2 was fitted with the usual six-spoke gold-painted aluminium FPS wheels with six-bolt disc attachments. However, the S2's 280mm discs had a different drilled pattern; no longer spiralled, the holes were drilled in groups of two followed by three and were in one piece, without detachable carriers. Only 900 S2s received these brake discs, although some also received the earlier discs with the alloy carriers. Tyres on all 1982 S2s were Pirelli Phantoms, an MT29 100/90V18 on the front and an MT28 110/90V18 on the rear.

There was no change to the specification of the front brake callipers, except that because the Brembo callipers were positioned behind the fork legs the brake lines were now all rubber, without the metal pipe connection. More changes occurred to the rear brake set-up. Since the brake had first been moved to the right side back in 1976, the exposed fluid reservoir had always looked an afterthought, but with the 900 S2 it was finally placed remotely behind the side cover where the regulator had previously been. The regulator now went up under the steering head with the electronic ignition components. The rear master cylinder was connected directly to the aluminium brake lever and this was a far neater solution than on previous models.

Folding footpegs (with rubbers) slotted into lugs on the frame and were more easily positioned, such details showing that Ducati had come a long way in the development of these bikes. There was a new rear-set gearshift lever, now with a removable end pin, but the gearshift linkage still included one ball joint and one clevis pin.

The 900 S2 continued into 1983 initially in the same bronze/grey colours, but soon received black bodywork and a red frame. As before both kick and electric start versions were built, 180 and 202 respectively. During the year there were some significant alterations to the kickstart engine, occurring after engine number 096314. These modifications did not affect the 900 S2 electric-start engines until 1984, as there was a backlog of engines left over from the Darmah. While the revised engine featured new crankcases, the square-case engine side covers were retained, together with the wet clutch. Visibly the alterations were easy to see as there was now a spin-on oil-filter and an oil level sight glass on the right-side crankcase.

With the red frame came a new centre-stand, now 900 SD-style rather than Super Sport, and a red chainguard. There was no longer a folding handle on the left side, the shape of the muffler bracket being altered instead to act as a handle. While all the bodywork was now painted black, the orange decals remained, as did the yellow, orange and red stripes. The front forks continued unchanged, but at the rear the 900 S2 received grey-bodied Marzocchi remote-reservoir shock absorbers.

At the end of 1983 an updated 900 S2 was displayed at the Bologna show. Still black with a red frame, this bike featured an interesting addition, a belly-pan under the engine. In a departure from the production 900 S2, but like the 900 Replica, the wheels were Oscam, with tubeless Michelin A48/M48 tyres. These would eventually feature on the 900 S2 later in 1984.

When it comes to categorisation of Ducati bevel-twins, 1984 is the most difficult year, and the 900 S2 epitomised these inconsistencies. Only the electric-start versions of the 900 S2 continued into 1984, and barely 205 were built. Some left-over

During 1983–84 some 900 S2s were black with red frames. This is a 1984 model with a belly-pan, while behind is a 900 SD Darmah and two 900 Mike Hailwood Replicas.

kickstart engines also had an electric start fitted, these receiving electric-start engine numbers. There was also considerable inconsistency in the internal engine specification from late 1983 into 1984, probably due to there being more engines than complete motorcycles produced during 1983. To further add to the confusion there was no official documentation indicating

This 1984 900 S2 has an engine with both a kick and electric start, although it has an electric-start engine number. Most 1984 900 S2s also had the spin-on oil-filter. This bike would originally have had a belly-pan.

which electric-start engines had the modified oil-filter. Some 907600 engines had these modifications, but some 907700 series engines did not.

The modifications to the electric-start versions paralleled those for the kickstart engines, and included the spin-on oil-filter and oil level sight glass in the right crankcase. Whereas the electric-start Hailwood Replica engine now incorporated the oil-filler in the right engine side cover, the 900 S2 continued with the earlier dipstick and plug on the left crankcase half.

There was a new frame designation for electric-start versions for late 1983 and 1984, now with a DM 900 S2 prefix and a new number sequence beginning at 095001. The kickstart 900 S2 of 1983 had a different frame number designation, DM 900 SS, and these numbers continued in the previous 092000 sequence but with an 'A' instead of '0' prefix, starting around A92400. The numbering of these frames was less straightforward than expected because the final DM 860 SS frames of 1983 had moved into the 092700 series before becoming DM 900 S2 095000. There seems to be no simple explanation for this particularly complicated frame classification.

Apart from the number designation, the red-painted frame was unchanged from 1983. The biggest alterations for the following year were to the colour scheme and graphics, most 1984 900 S2s having new bodywork, now painted red, with silver stripes in three shades. Some 900 S2s still had the black paintwork and tank decals of the earlier year, but with the later engine. The rectangular CEV front indicators were no longer flush-mounted in the fairing, but were mounted on stalks. A belly-pan, as had appeared on the earlier show bike, made it to the production versions but was red, or black, in line with the rest of the bodywork, and was not a particularly useful feature – a severe case of form over function.

The first 1984 900 S2s had six-spoke gold-painted FPS aluminium wheels shod with Pirelli Phantom tyres. Later, with the revised engine with the spin-on oil-filter, came the Oscam wheels of the 1983–84

Mike Hailwood Replica and their Michelin A48/M48 tubeless tyres. These final 900 S2s featured the unreliable vacuum fuel taps and black fuel lines of the 1983–84 900 Replica. Also shared with the 900 Replica was the instrument panel, which had a new plastic warning light console. While the Marzocchi forks were still the same as the previous year, with the external dust seals, the red 1984 S2s had air caps in the top of the fork legs.

Production of the 900 S2 had finished by around frame number 096000, only 1,236 being constructed, of which 353 were kick-

Only 205 900 S2s were manufactured in 1984, about half of them red with plastic tank badges instead of orange decals. Most 1984 S2s also came with the Oscam wheels of the Mike Hailwood Replica.

start versions. Although only a qualified success, it was the S2, rather than the proven Super Sport, that was to form the basis of the final bevel-gear Ducatis. In retrospect this was a mistake. While there were some genuine improvements in the execution of Taglioni's magnificent design, the basic chassis was inferior.

CHAPTER 9

Bigger and better?

The year 1983 was a very uncertain time at Ducati. Morale was at a low point, and a deal with Cagiva in Varese to supply Pantah engines was in the offing. By the end of 1982, 3,796 kickstart Mike Hailwood Replicas had been manufactured, and engine numbers were in the 096000 series. While the kickstart 900 Mike Hailwood Replica continued through into early 1983 unchanged from its 1982 form, it soon featured the completely revised chassis and running gear of the 900 S2. Now considerably taller, heavier and larger than the earlier Super Sport-derived bikes, one benefit was superior ground clearance. However, these 900s did not steer or handle as well as the earlier type, and the frame was largely to blame. Weakness in the area around the battery led to the Replica (and 900 S2) being less stable and prone to steering oscillation.

The kickstart engine was still the square-case 860, identical to the kickstart 900 S2, but soon there would be a completely revised electric-start engine. The most serious revision since the square-case of 1974, this appeared in September 1983. While somewhat overshadowed by the Mille engine of a year later, these final 900s were the smoothest and best developed of all the 860 engines. Their smoothness rivalled that of the earlier 750, with production and quality at the factory much more consistent than it had been even a year earlier. Unfortunately it was to be a victim of

economics and circumstance and would not feature a long production run.

The kickstart Mike Hailwood Replica continued into early 1983, with frame numbers still carrying the DM 900 R designation and numbers well into the 904000 series. Production was still relatively healthy, with 780 produced in 1983. A few months later the revised version appeared, and even though the red-painted frame shared little with the previous model, the frame number sequence continued as before. There was a new prefix, DM 900 R1, with the numbers for the revised electric start version beginning at 905002 (905001 was a pre-production show bike). As the kickstart (and few square-case electric start) Mike Hailwood Replica numbers finished at 904719 there was a small gap in the number sequence. The kickstart engines of the 1983 Replica continued from about engine number DM860 095700 and were shared with the 900 S2, the same modifications affecting these engines that were detailed in the previous chapter. By the end of 1983 nearly all the 900 Mike Hailwood Replicas would come with the new electric-start motor (only 25 kickstart MHRs being built in 1984). In line with the electric-start 900 S2, these now used the number sequence for electric-start desmodromic engines that had begun with the 900 SD back in 1977. This was up to the DM860 907000 series during 1983, with the revised electric-start Mike Hailwood Replica beginning at around 907800. As production did not begin until September, fewer electric-start Replicas (687) were made than kick-starts in 1983.

While the desmodromic cylinder heads were unchanged from the 900 S2, there were a number of significant changes to the rest of the engine. By now both the valve seats and valve guides were cast iron, the cast-iron guides now being identical for both inlet and exhaust valves. The new Mille was also being developed at this time and many of its features were incorporated in the 900 Replica, which would be a test-ing ground before the introduction of the Mille.

There were new crankcases again, also with the oil level sight glass incorporated in the right crankcase half, and the spin-on oil-filter that had featured on the final square-case engines. A gutter near the secondary shaft bearing now redirected oil splashed from the primary drive on to the secondary shaft. The shape of both engine side covers was restyled away from the angular Giugiaro square-case. While not as attrac-tive as the earlier round-case, some effort had been made to integrate the electric start into the left-side cover. The right-side alter-nator cover carried a black plastic oil-filler

plug, and a removable plate to allow for ignition timing setting. This had to be moved from the clutch side because the new clutch cover was in two parts. The new covers would carry though to the Mille.

The crankshaft specification was as before but there was a change to the pistons and cylinders. While the bore size remained at 86mm, with 20 x 59mm gudgeon pins, the cylinders no longer had removable cast-iron liners. In line with the 500 and 600 SL Pantah, the cylinders and liners were now in one piece, and coated with 'Gilnisil', an Italian 'Nikisil'. These could not be rebored, but the wear rates were much lower than with cast iron.

The primary drive and clutch were completely revised. While the helical-geared primary drive ratio was unchanged at 32/70, the gears were new. The 32-tooth crankshaft gear bolted to a lighter flywheel, while the 70-tooth clutch gear, mounted on the mainshaft, sat inside the outer case cover that contained the ignition pick-ups

The author's 900 MHR in 1984. As the lower half of the fairing was removed to aid ground clearance, the new engine cases are clearly seen. The footpegs are non-standard, as are the Conti mufflers.

and electric start. The clutch was now dry and covered by another case cover, this time polished aluminium. The design also followed that of the Pantah, the six driven plates being metal, and the seven driving plates having friction surfaces. The outer pressure plate was also metal, and there were stronger clutch springs. As the method of actuation changed from cable to hydraulic, stronger springs were not a problem.

The gearbox was the same three-dog type that had been fitted to the later 1982 engines, but for a new mainshaft with first and second gears, and a new 30-tooth driving gear. This mainshaft carried different splines to locate the new inner clutch drum and two internal O-rings to seal the clutch-operating mechanism. With the clutch cover now in two parts, the electric start motor and ignition pick-ups were mounted on the inner cover. The starter motor was now a much smaller and lighter 12-volt/0.7kW Nippon Denso unit, and reasonably reliable on the 900, more so than the later Mille. With the Bosch ignition

Some 1983–84 900 Replicas came with a two-into-one Conti exhaust on the left, leaving the right side bare. This is a contemporary road test shot. (Two Wheels)

pick-ups still in the engine oil, these were mounted on a plate that allowed for easy setting of individual air gaps. As with the previous Bosch BTZ ignition systems, a four-stage advance was used, with slightly less maximum advance than before, at 28°. The trend towards less advance had been a gradual one over the years, coinciding with better ignition systems.

Carburation and air filtration followed the 900 S2. Two identical (front) inlet manifolds were used, so the rear carburettor would clear the larger battery the Dell'Orto PHM 40 BD/BS carburettors using twin air-filters. These filters were remarkably efficient, and the 1983–84 series of 900 Mike Hailwood Replicas was one of the strongest-performing bevel-twin Ducatis.

Also shared with the S2 were the exhaust pipes. Both the standard Silentium and optional Conti mufflers had brackets further back to fit the S2 frame. Some 1984 900 Mike Hailwood Replicas came with a Conti two-into-one exhaust system, the muffler (with removable baffles) on the left side. Generally, however, the 1983–84 Hailwood Replicas were fitted with the Silentium mufflers with the Contis listed as an option.

Very few frame and cycle parts were shared with the 1982 Hailwood Replica.

The fairing was completely revised, and now much narrower and taller. The 1983 kickstart Replica had a different fairing, screen and indicators from the electric-start version; the fairing was now separated horizontally across the white stripe, making access to the engine considerably easier. Ground clearance was improved, but the lower fairing still grounded relatively easily. The right fuel tap was now a vacuum type connected to the front inlet manifold. In typical Ducati fashion, as if they distrusted it, the left tap was manual. In retrospect Ducati was right, because the vacuum taps were very prone to leaking. The fuel lines were black rubber instead of the green plastic that had served so well for many years.

With the completely new fairing came revised decals, and the front indicators were no longer flush mounted. A new design of side cover featured on the 1983 Replica. Constructed of ABS, these had a white '900' decal, while on the red seat unit (and solo seat cover) there were also new green decals. The only interchangeable body parts with the earlier version were the solo seat cover and seat pad.

The few 1983 Replicas fitted with either a square-case electric-start or kickstart engine still used the instruments, headlight and handlebars of the 900 S2; these were a Darmah-style instrument panel, Bosch headlight, and forward-offset chromed clip-on handlebars with black levers. The clutch was still operated by a cable on all square-case engines. Many more of the 1983–84 Hailwood Replicas came with the new electric-start engine, and with this there were quite a number of significant changes.

With the new engine and its hydraulically actuated clutch came new handlebars, headlight, and a completely new instrument panel. Even though the instruments were the Nippon Denso that had been used from the Darmah of 1977, there was a new set of warning lights. There was also a new 170mm 60-watt H4 Carello headlight. New Verlicchi black anodised forward-offset clip-on handlebars were used on Replicas featuring the revised instrument panel, which provided a much wider range of adjustment than the earlier type. A Brembo hydraulic clutch master cylinder sat on the left handlebar, with the regular rubber Verlicchi handgrips. The 1983 Replicas with the revised engine and instrument panel had dog-leg brake and clutch levers.

The revised Replica had a new instrument panel, handlebars and hydraulic clutch. The Verlicchi throttle incorporated an electric start and engine stop switch.

The Nippon Denso switch gear, Verlicchi plastic twin-cable throttle incorporating the electric start and engine stop button, and the large rectangular CEV taillight and rear indicators were straight off the 900 S2. The front indicators came from the 650 SL Pantah of the same era and were not the most attractive items.

There were new forks, shock absorbers, wheels and brakes for the 1983 Replica, most of which were changed to follow fashionable trends, but there were a couple of genuine improvements. The black-painted Marzocchi forks located the Brembo brake callipers behind the fork legs rather than in front. While all the fork legs were painted black on these 900 Replicas, during 1984 they were painted matt black rather than the earlier crinkle finish.

The 38 x 590mm fork tubes, with a 221mm hydraulic brake rod, were also similar to the S2 but with internal dust seals. The final 1984 900 Replicas featured air caps on top of the forks. At the rear came new 330mm (13-inch) black-bodied oleo-pneumatic Marzocchi shock absorbers. The black chainguard, identical to that of the 1972–74 750 Sport, made a return for 1983–84.

New wheels also graced the 1983 and 1984 900 Replica. While the gold-painted aluminium Oscam wheels were the same size as the earlier FPS, MT 2.15 x 18 inches on the front and MT 2.50 x 18 inches on the rear, they now took tubeless tyres, Michelin M48, 100/90V18 and 120/90V18. The front mudguard was black ABS, the same shape as the 1982 Replica and Super Sport. Essentially the Brembo brakes were unchanged; the 280mm drilled discs with six-bolt alloy carriers were the same, as were the black 08 Brembo brake callipers. Following on from the 900 S2, the rear brake master cylinder now used a remote fluid reservoir, located under the right-side cover. The folding footpegs (with rubbers) and aluminium levers also came from the 900 S2.

The left side of an unrestored 1984 900 Mike Hailwood Replica. This bike originally came with Silentium mufflers and internal fork dust seals but otherwise is standard.

In all, 1,457 of these revised Mike Hailwood Replicas were built between September 1983 and July 1984, 770 in the latter year, when they were superseded by the Mille. Although overshadowed by the new bike, in some respects the final 900 was a more refined machine. The engine gave away little in maximum power and more than made up for the slightly reduced mid-range with increased smoothness and

tractability. It was a pity that the chassis and running gear did not receive the attention and development given to the engine.

The 1983 updated 900 Mike Hailwood Replica was always considered a stopgap model while a new engine was being developed by Fabio Taglioni and his new assistant, Ing. Massimo Bordi. Well before the 1983 agreement with Cagiva, Taglioni had been given the go-ahead by VM management to update the bevel-gear engine, and it finally materialised in mid-1984, looking visually identical to the revised 900; when placed in the chassis of the 1983 900 Replica, it was difficult to distinguish between the two. However, inside the Mille engine there were a number of important differences, and these contributed to the engine's distinctly different characteristics.

Mille engines can be differentiated from

Another view of the 1984 900 MHR. The tail light and indicators were shared with the S2 and 650 SL Pantah. (Roy Kidney)

their 860 cousins by another set of engine numbers. These started at ZDM1000 100001, and the number series for the Mille Replica was shared with the Mille S2. The crankcases were new, and easily visually identified by a larger spin-on oil-filter with an oil pressure switch nearby. With fewer engine parts shared between the Mille and square-case 860, this final redesign was almost as significant as the square-case had been in 1974. However, this time there was no racing engine as a precedent. The Mille never had any pretensions as a racing design, those duties having been successfully entrusted to the newer Pantah.

Unlike the 860, the increase in capacity to 973cc was gained not only through boring the engine, but also stroking it. The bore was only increased 2mm, to 88mm, but the stroke was increased to 80mm. The big changes came with the crankshaft, which now followed Pantah practice by being forged in one piece, and using two-piece plain big-end bearings. Despite the

5.6mm increase in stroke, the eye-to-eye length of the con-rod was unchanged at 145mm. Thus the con-rod-to-stroke ratio was reduced even further for the Mille, to 1.81:1. This contributed even more to mid-range power, but was undoubtedly done to keep engine height the same as before.

Because the con-rods were now in two pieces with plain bearings, the crankshaft journal size was increased to 45mm, with a corresponding increase in rigidity. If only Ducati could have given the bevel-twin the Mille crank earlier the engine may have had a longer production run. As with the Pantah, Mille crankshafts did not break, and big-end problems were a thing of the past. There were no changes to the fibre-caged ball main bearings or main bearing housings, which remained the same as had been fitted to every bevel-twin from the 750 GT.

Whereas the 900 revision of the primary drive and clutch in 1983 had been quite extensive, the Mille went even further. For the first time since the 1974 750 Super Sport, a production Ducati twin had a primary drive ratio that was not 32/70. The Mille helical primary gear ratio sped the clutch up even faster with 39- and 69-tooth gears (1.769:1). The hydraulically operated dry clutch was largely unchanged, except for a new outside pressure disc and clutch springs.

The Nippon Denso electric start motor was also carried over, and for the Mille received a new crankshaft gear and drive pinion, giving a lower drive ratio. There was no doubt that Taglioni and Bordi had expected the bigger engine to be more difficult to turn over, but even the lower gearing was insufficient to help the small electric motor. Combined with the added friction of the thick oil and plain bearings, the Mille engine could be an especially reluctant starter, which was its most serious problem.

After engine number 100388 Mille engines used a new oil pump, with a larger body, providing increased flow. There were new oil pump drive gears and timing gear bearing support plate, the crankshaft timing gear no longer incorporating the smaller secondary oil pump gear. Because of the wider oil pump body, the pump was now driven directly off the central crankshaft gear. As the Mille used a full-flow oil-filter system, there was a pressure relief valve and spring inside the right crankcase, underneath the oil-filter, and a larger filter was used. From engine number 100129 the front cylinder received an oil flow reducing plug. Right to the end, the bevel-twins used the same labyrinth engine crankcase breather, which screwed into the right rear crankcase half.

The Mille received new shifting forks within the gear selector mechanism. Most of the gears and shafts were also altered, the secondary shaft and primary shaft carrying a closer-ratio gearbox, still with three engagement dogs. These final gearboxes were indicative of the improving quality at Borgo Panigale, being vastly improved over earlier versions even if the same could not be said for the assembly quality. The only gear carried over from previous gearboxes was the 22-tooth secondary shaft fifth gear. First gear was raised considerably to 1:2.720, second up to 1:1.761 and third to 1:1.250. Fourth remained a direct drive and fifth a 1:0.887 reduction.

The camshaft drive and desmodromic camshafts were unchanged from before, as were the basic cylinder heads. Thus, despite the Pantah now using a 60° included valve angle, the 80° valve angle was retained. The larger engine did receive bigger inlet valves, at 42mm, but the exhaust valve was still 36mm, and there were new cast-iron valve seats.

Carburation was also carried over from the 1983 900 Replica, with two Dell'Orto

The frontal aspect of the Mille was the same as the 1984 900 Replica, with a taller and narrower fairing than on earlier models. (Two Wheels)

Externally the Mille engine looked very similar to the 1984 900 MHR, but internally there were many changes. (Two Wheels)

PHM 40 BD/BS carburettors with twin-pleated paper air-filters in metal housings. The carburettor jetting was the same as for the 900, but less satisfactory. Whereas the 900 carburation was glitch-free, the Mille had a tendency to hunt on part throttle. This was an area that really required further development, again indicating that the Mille had been hastily put into production. It was almost as if Taglioni feared the worst with the impending Cagiva take-over and was determined to get the Mille out as soon as possible.

Only Silentium mufflers were specified, but Contis with the more rearward bracket would bolt straight on, as would the two-into-one Conti system. Although not listed in the official literature, the factory publicity brochure claims an increase to 90bhp at 7,500rpm with the two-into-one exhaust system and short bell mouths.

The red-painted frame of the Mille Replica was identical to that of the final 900 Replica, but carried a new frame number sequence. These now had a ZDM 1000R prefix with numbers beginning at 100001. Apart from the engine, there were very few differences between the Mille and the previous 900 Replica. Visually the Mille was identifiable by 'Mille' or sometimes '1000' decals on the fairing, underneath the 'Mike Hailwood Replica' decals. Only a few of the earliest Milles had the '1000' decal. The '900' on the side covers was replaced by a 'DESMO' decal. The front mudguard was now red rather than black and most Mille Replicas had a black lockable fuel tank filler cap.

Even though they looked identical, and were the same length, the 38mm Marzocchi forks were also new for the Mille. Still with the rear-mounted Brembo brake callipers, the fork legs were initially painted black, then later red. The triple clamps were also painted red on those Mille Replicas with red forks, but the red did not match that of

Only the 'Mille' decals distinguish the Mille Replica from the 900. Later versions had red-painted fork legs.

the frame and bodywork. All Milles received air caps in the top of the fork tubes and these required new 590mm tubes. While the 18-inch Oscam aluminium wheels were also carried over from the final 900 Replica, there was a new cush drive flange. The Mille's tyres were again tubeless Michelin M48s, the rear increasing to a 130/80V18.

During 1984 the Mille engine also replaced the 900 in the S2. While they looked quite different, the Mille Replica and Mille S2 were essentially identical, the latter being more closely related to the Replica than the earlier 900 S2. Engines were shared and used the same number sequence starting with ZDM1000 100001. However, as the Mille S2 went into production a few months after the Mille Replica, their engine numbers started at around 100500, and included the later engine modifications such as the revised oil pump.

The red-painted Mille S2 and Mille

All Mille S2s were black with red frames and orange decals, although most had 'Mille' rather than '1000' side cover decals. Apart from the bodywork, the S2 was identical to the Replica.

Replica frames were identical, but carried different number sequences; for the S2 the frame number designation was ZDM 1000 S2, starting at 100001. Although the running gear was also identical between the two models, the Mille S2 only had the red-painted Marzocchi forks with air caps. While the Replica had a red front mudguard, that of the Mille S2 was black, and although a prototype Mille S2 had run with 16-inch Campagnolo wheels, the production machines had the same 18-inch wheels, brakes, tyres and rear Marzocchi shock absorbers as the Mille Replica. Also shared with the Mille Replica were the instrument panel, Carello headlight, Verlicchi clip-on handlebars, and hydraulic clutch and master cylinder with black dog-leg levers.

The bodywork of the Mille S2 was, however, essentially a 1983 900 S2. The fairing, fuel tank, seat and side covers were black with the earlier yellow, orange and red stripes, and the flush-mounted lockable fuel tank cap and right vacuum fuel tap were retained. As with the 1984 900 S2 there was a belly-pan mounted underneath the engine, painted black to match the rest

This 1985 Mille prototype has a 16-inch wheel and a square headlight. Photographed in a dark corner of the factory during 1997, bikes like this are now displayed in the museum.

of the bodywork. The large CEV taillight and indicators were also carried through from the 1984 900 S2.

Production of the Mille S2 was short-lived, and with only 171 constructed (71 in 1984 and 100 in 1985) they were certainly one of the rarer members of the bevel-twin family. With the Cagiva take-over the Mille Replica was given a brief reprise, but the S2 was discontinued almost immediately.

The Mille was pure contradiction. In many ways it was vastly improved over the 750 and 860 twins, yet somehow it missed the mark. By 1984 the production quality had improved dramatically but, unfortunately for the Mille, production coincided with the Cagiva purchase of the company and this saw a downturn in quality leading to 1985. Without doubt the Mille engine could have been the most reliable of all the bevel engines, but it really needed more development, and a more up-to-date chassis.

In early 1985 a Mille prototype, in red and yellow like the factory F2 racers, was constructed, and by mid-1985 a more radical replacement Mille Replica was being tested. This was also red and yellow, and drew on some of the parts of the 750 F1,

notably a 16-inch front wheel and square headlight. Front forks were Marzocchi M1R. Production of this bike did not, however, materialise, and later in 1985 a Mille Replica appeared with the Cagiva (an elephant) logo. Prior to this, Massimo Tamburini had designed a box-section aluminium frame for the Mille. Also with Marzocchi M1R forks, this featured 16-inch wheels front and rear and rising rate rear suspension. Again nothing happened, but eventually this chassis formed the basis of the Paso. While 662 were built in 1984, only 200 Mille Replicas left the factory in 1985, and the model was discontinued early in 1986, a final 250 Mike Hailwood Replicas being built to use up the stock of pre-built engines; this made a total of 1,112 constructed. If circumstances had been different the Mille could have survived, but unfortunately by 1986 production of the wonderful bevel-gear engine had become an uneconomic proposition.

CHAPTER 10

Resurrection

When Cagiva purchased Ducati in 1985 they halted the company's downward slide. Undoubtedly those final years under the VM banner were almost catastrophic, with low production and variable quality. With Cagiva, not only did the quality improve immediately, but so also did the emphasis. Cagiva saw Ducati's salvation in motorcycles with a broader appeal, and there was soon a move away from pure sporting bikes. With the demise of the bevel-gear engine, the entire range would be based on Taglioni's Pantah with camshafts driven by toothed rubber belts. Initially starting life as a 500 in 1979, this design was so advanced that it was easily able to accommodate repeated increases in displacement and still maintain reliability levels far in excess of any bevel-gear twin. The fact that it is still in production as a 600, virtually unchanged, indicates the excellence of the design.

A large proportion of Pantahs were sporting models. Indeed, the Pantah had started life as the 500 SL, but it was not really a Super Sport in the usual Ducati context. The SL series was not race-derived and had some serious deficiencies, particularly frame rigidity. However, it soon evolved into one of the all-time classic racing Ducatis, the 600cc TT2, and this was to become the ancestor for the next series of Super Sport.

Not only was the TT2 a classic design, but it could also claim to be one of the most successful racing Ducatis ever. After Tony Rutter won the TT Formula 2 event at the Isle of Man in 1981 on a Sports Motorcycles-prepared and modified 500 SL, Ducati entered the fray with a factory TT2 racer. These bikes went on to dominate domestic and international TT2 events throughout 1982, Rutter winning his second TT2 World Championship, which he followed up with further titles in 1983 and 1984. With the possibility of the TT2 World Championship disappearing, development of a 750cc TT1 version was hastened during 1984. Initially these shared the cantilever swing-arm rear suspension of the TT2, but soon factory bikes had more sophisticated rising rate rear suspension. TT1s were campaigned in F1 and Endurance events from 1984 until 1986, but could not repeat the success of the TT2.

As had happened earlier, these racing bikes spawned street replicas, and even if they did not carry the Super Sport label, they were undoubtedly a Super Sport in spirit. Unfortunately, when the 750 F1 appeared during 1985 it disappointed many enthusiasts hoping for an up-to-date race replica. The red frame was based on the earlier 600 TT2, so had cantilever rear suspension, but probably the most unsatisfactory feature was the use of an Oscam 16-inch front wheel. In concert with an 18-inch rear, the rim sizes of the gold-painted wheels were increased to 2.50 and 3.00 inches and mounted with the usual slippery

Michelin A48/M48 tyres, 120/80V16 and 130/80V18.

To differentiate the F1 from earlier 750s, engine numbers began at ZDM 750 7500001, with frame numbers also at 7500001. Despite revised camshafts, engine performance was barely improved over earlier 750s as the first F1 used 500 cylinder heads with 37.5 and 33.5mm valves; as with all Pantahs, these were inclined at 60°. Carburation was by means of the usual Dell'Orto PHF 36 AD/AS carburettors, with small individual foam filters, there not being enough space within the confines of the racing frame for anything else. The F1 had an oil-cooler mounted in the front of the fairing, but this was a crude bypass system to the cylinder heads that used cheap rubber tubing with crimped metal clamps. There was also a new Conti two-into-one exhaust system that contributed to the excellent mid-range power characteristics of the F1.

Where the F1 did succeed was as a light, narrow and compact sporting motorcycle. Rolling on a 1,400mm (55-inch) wheelbase, the 175kg (385lb) bike was significantly smaller than earlier Super Sports, especially when compared to the final truck-like Mike

Hailwood Replicas. Many parts were, however, shared with those contemporary bikes, including the Nippon Denso instruments and switches, Verlicchi handlebars and throttle, Bosch ignition, and the same Brembo brakes and hydraulic clutch. The 1985 750 F1 used basic red-painted Marzocchi forks with air caps, but fully floating cast-iron disc brakes, 280mm on the front and 260mm at the rear.

Styling followed that of the TT2 with an aluminium fuel tank, full fairing and solo seat. It was not the most successful exercise as the large seat unit needed to hide the rear-mounted battery, and somehow the square headlight looked out of place. The hand-beaten fuel tank featured a quick release, and was vented into the left handlebar. This was the final Ducati to feature the old-style Giugiaro graphics, and engine numbers went to about 7500500.

Even with the Cagiva take-over, there was a revised F1 for 1986, production starting in late 1985. While essentially

The direct descendent of the magnificent TT2 racing bikes was the 750 F1. The 1985 version was the final Ducati to feature the Giugiaro graphics.

A slightly revised 750 F1 appeared in 1986, incorporating some significant engine improvements and a slightly restyled seat. (Streetbike)

unchanged, this did much to redress some of the criticisms of the earlier model, but in the process some of the nicer touches disappeared. The fully floating rear disc went, and the aluminium fuel tank made way for one of steel. In every other respect, however, the 1986 model was improved over the earlier version. The engine received new crankcases, with a stronger dry clutch, straight-cut primary gears and a new gearbox – no longer was the F1 merely a beefed-up 500. In the cylinder head there were new camshafts, and finally larger valves, 41 and 35mm. There was also a much improved full-flow oil-cooling system.

While the shape of the fairing was the same, the seat was successfully restyled. More important alterations came with the 40mm Forcella Italia forks and white-faced Veglia instruments, which would feature on sporting Ducatis for the next 11 years. There was no change to the Oscam wheels, except that they were painted red. Now

with Cagiva-inspired graphics, the 1986 F1 had elephant logos on the fairing and tank. Even though the bike was available well into 1988 in some markets, they were all manufactured in 1986.

Significantly, however, there was a limited edition F1 available during 1986, called the Montjuich in honour not only of Ducati's many victories there over the years, but specifically for Grau, de Juan and Reyes's win in the non-championship 24 Hour race of 1983. First appearing at the Milan show at the end of 1985, only 200 Montjuichs were constructed, each carrying a numbered plaque. They also shared the regular 750 F1 engine and frame number sequence.

The Montjuich differed considerably from the regular F1. While the bottom end of the engine was identical, except for the crankcases and longer gearbox shafts, there were a number of changes to the top end of the engine. New valves came with even wilder camshafts, breathing through Dell'Orto PMH 40ND/NS carburettors. Although the pistons (and hence the compression ratio) were the same, the

Montjuich received stronger cylinder head studs. Ignition on all Montjuichs was Japanese Kokusan, and the dry clutch had a vented cover. Completing the performance package was an indecently loud Verlicchi competition exhaust system.

Using the same F1 frame but without a centrestand, the Montjuich received an alloy swing-arm but still retained the cantilever suspension. A higher-quality Marzocchi rear suspension unit was used, although the Forcella Italia front forks were identical. Fully floating Brembo disc rotors were fitted all round, the front brakes being four-piston racing Brembo 'Goldline'. There was a departure with the wheels, too, with 16-inch composite aluminium Marvic wheels fitted front and rear, in much wider sizes than before. These allowed for racing Michelin intermediate tyres, 12/60 x 16 and 18/67 x 16. The fuel tank was again hand-beaten aluminium, and a racing aerodynamic front mudguard was used. Rather than red, white and green, the Montjuich was finished in the traditional NCR racing colours of red and silver. Undoubtedly this was a true race replica in the tradition of the first 750 Super Sport, the only blemish being the 16-inch wheels. Soon the 750 F1 began to incorporate some of the Montjuich features. From engine number 7501495 the

gearboxes and crankcases were uniform, and all ignition systems became Kokusan. The very last F1s, after engine 7502169, had a revised clutch slave cylinder, bearing and clutch cover.

The true heirs to the Super Sport spirit were, however, the limited edition F1s, and there was another for 1987, the Laguna Seca (also built at the end of 1986). Named this time in honour of Marco Lucchinelli's victory in the Battle of the Twins race at that racetrack in 1986, each of the 200 Laguna Secas carried his signature. History repeated itself with this bike. Just as the 1976 Super Sport had been softened, so was the Laguna Seca. There were no engine changes apart from a new exhaust system, but the aluminium fuel tank went, alongside the light composite Marvic wheels. Now with the 16-inch Oscam wheels and disc rotors straight off the Paso, fortunately the racing Brembo callipers were retained. The two handlebar master cylinders were now rectangular, although the regular 750 F1 continued with the earlier type. The different wheels also required a revised rear

Highly desirable limited edition F1s were produced from 1986 to 1988. Here is a Laguna Seca from 1987 and a Montjuich from 1986. (Streetbike)

brake set-up. While the Laguna Seca received a new front mudguard, the F1 now had the guard of the Montjuich. By now all F1s had a dual seat, and this also appeared on some Laguna Secas. Completing the revision was a lower fairing screen and a swing-arm-attached mudguard over the rear wheel. The fairing decals lost the Cagiva elephant, but it was still retained on the fuel tank.

Amazingly, given Cagiva's preoccupation with the Paso, a third limited edition F1 was offered for 1988 (although they were built in late 1987). These would be the final Ducatis without reversed rear cylinder heads. This new limited edition F1 was called the Santa Monica, after the Misano circuit where Marco Lucchinelli had scored a surprising victory in the World Championship Formula 1 race of 1986. Now only with a dual seat, the Santa Monica had a red and white colour scheme and reverted to the 16-inch wheels and fully floating disc brakes of the Montjuich. All the engine specifications were as before, and the Santa Monica also featured a numbered plaque.

Flawed the F1s may have been, but they were nevertheless race replicas in the best Ducati tradition. Cagiva had hoped that the 750 Paso would replace the F1, but as it was such a radical departure it alienated many traditional Ducati buyers. Unfortunately the F1 was an expensive motorcycle to produce, the limited edition versions even more so. Cagiva had no real plans to keep it in production and if it had not been for the spectacular failure of the Paso the F1 would probably have finished in 1985. As it was, the F1s, in any of their incarnations (including the 350/400 F3), were the last traditional Ducati and still built in relatively small numbers: the total made from 1985 to 1987 (including the limited edition variants) was only 2,205. Built only to cater for anomalies in the Italian and Japanese markets, the under-powered F3 does not really qualify as a Super Sport, and is outside the scope of this book. However, these were also built in very small numbers, 976 in 1986, plus a final 200 six-speed 400s in late 1988 for the Japanese market.

With the demise of the bevel-gear engine Cagiva's programme centred on the development of the Pantah, the first alteration being to reverse the cylinder heads to enable the use of a Weber automotive-style carburettor. For better or worse Cagiva were totally committed to this concept and soon incorporated it in an F1 replacement, the 750 Sport of 1988. Combining the engine and exhaust system of the 750 Paso in a modified 750 F1 steel trellis frame, it failed to recreate the soul of its namesake, the classic 750 Sport of 1972–74.

Although not a Super Sport, the *nuovo* 750 Sport was important because, as with its earlier namesake, it paved the way for the next generation of Super Sport. Because of the use of the Weber 44DCNF113 carburettor and large airbox, the F1 frame needed to be considerably revised to accommodate it, leading to a new fuel tank incorporating a fuel filter and pump. The cantilever swing-arm was an aluminium type similar to that on the limited edition F1s, but with low-spec Marzocchi suspension was used front and rear. The 16-inch wheels and brakes were also straight from the Paso. At a time when 16-inch wheels were losing popularity this seemed a backward step.

The first 750 Sports of July 1988 were blue and red (now without elephant logos), and suffered a series of problems, particularly cracking swing-arms and carburettor glitches. However, already production was up to F1 levels, with 1,241 constructed in 1988. Only a few months later a revised red and silver version was displayed at the Cologne show. Although not actually available until mid-1989, this incorporated some significant improvements, particularly with additional oil-cooling jackets around the cylinders. Some 750 Sports were also made in black and silver, and production was 965 in 1989, with a mere 153 during 1990. The *nuovo* Sport was not Ducati's best effort, but late in 1989 a far more successful variant appeared, the resurrected 900 Super Sport, its name now styled as a single word, Supersport. All new-generation Super Sports would now be either an SS or Supersport.

Cagiva endeavoured to recreate the 750 Sport during 1988, but the result was disappointing. Let down by 16-inch wheels and a Weber carburettor, it failed to win the hearts of enthusiasts. (Two Wheels)

Although it had been mentioned in the press for some time, the 900 Supersport did not finally make an appearance until October 1989, as a 1990 model. Once again Ducati had created a hybrid, and as with all such designs it was not totally satisfactory. Into the 750 Sport frame went an air/oil-cooled engine derived from the recently introduced 906 Paso. Coupled with the running gear of the eight-valve 851, theoretically this was an ideal concoction, but although they constructed 1,471 in 1989, and a further 533 during 1990, unfortunately Ducati still did not get it right.

With the 906 Paso, the 1989 Supersport was the first two-valve engine to receive the new-generation 'large crankcase' design of the 851. This incorporated many changes to the Pantah design, notably a six-speed gearbox. The engine was, however, stroked 4mm over the 851 and received new conrods, with a 130mm eye-to-eye length. The big-end bearing size went up from the 40mm of the 750 to 42mm, and gudgeon size was also increased from 18 to 19mm. The hydraulically operated dry clutch was

as for the 851 of 1988 and the 1989 851 Corsa. Here the larger engines differed from the smaller Pantahs in that the hydraulic clutch control was on the left side, and could be removed keeping the fluid intact. One thing that would characterise Ducatis from now on was a myriad of clutch alterations to cope with the larger engines, but these affected the four-valve series more than the Supersport. The group of plates on the 900 Supersport consisted of seven steel, and seven fibre.

In the cylinder head, valve sizes increased to 43mm and 38mm, the two valves still having a 60° included angle. Feeding the cylinders was the Weber 44 DCNF 116 twin-choke carburettor, which continued to be a source of frustration, and the exhaust system was now from the 851 rather than the Paso. The Weber carburettor suffered from icing in severe and wet conditions, and

even as late as 1992 a carburettor heating kit that included a front cylinder cover and intakes became available.

For some reason the Kokusan ignition was replaced by a Marelli Digiplex (also shared with the 906), powered by a new 350-watt alternator. The air/oil cooling system was, however, a development of that of the 750 Sport, although cooling to the rear exhaust valve continued to be a problem.

With some extra bracing around the steering head, the red-painted frame now had a slightly steeper steering head angle of 27°. The 40mm Marzocchi front forks were still non-adjustable, and the single rear Marzocchi shock for spring pre-load only. Where the 900 SS did score in comparison with its earlier namesake was in its size. The dry weight of 180kg (396lb) was comparable, but the new bike rolled on a much shorter 1,450mm (57-inch) wheelbase, and on contemporary rubber.

Adopting the white Brembo 17-inch wheels from the 851 truly launched the bike into the late 1980s. Its thoroughly modern rim sizes of 3.50 and 5.50 inches were shod with new-generation radial tyres, either Pirelli or Michelin. It could have been argued that with the gigantic 180/55 ZR17 rear Michelin the 78bhp Supersport was over-tyred, but there was no denying that these were a vast improvement over the earlier 16-inch wheels.

The front brakes also came in for an upgrade. While the stainless steel disc rotors were only 300mm (the 851 received 320mm discs), they were gripped by Brembo four-piston callipers. These P4 32d brake callipers had two sets of 32mm pistons, operated by a PS15 master cylinder with a 15mm piston. The rear disc was from the 851, and down to 245mm. Here the 32mm twin-piston P2105N Brembo calliper was operated by a rear PS11 master cylinder with an 11mm piston.

Most other cycle parts were procured from the 750 Sport or 906 Paso, lights and white-faced Veglia instruments from the former, and the 906's switches and controls. Here Ducati had made undoubted progress

There was still something not quite right about the styling and balance of the 900 Supersport of 1990. (Two Wheels)

under Cagiva and the 900 Supersport seemed a generation in advance of the 750 F1 that had only finished production a year or so earlier.

Derived strongly from the 750 Sport, the red and white bodywork, with a solo seat cowling, looked striking but still lacked that unity that was always evident with the best Ducatis. Somehow the mating of the larger wheels with the earlier frame did not quite work. While they had been endeavouring to appeal to the traditionalist, Ducati had yet to hit the bull's-eye, and that would not happen until 1991.

11

The new classic Supersport

Within the history of Ducati there has always been the occasional vintage year, a year where the entire production line-up has been outstanding, 1974 was one of those years, and so was 1991. At the Cologne show of 1990 the spearhead of the 1991 line-up, a new 900 Supersport, was displayed. It still drew heavily on the 1990 version, but the changes made were significant and, what is more, looked totally new. With continual development, this Supersport would have a seven-year production run, almost rivalling the eight years of the first 900 SS.

Although much of the engine was the same as before, following on from the World Superbike racing programme, the large-crankcase engines of 1991 (851, 888 and 904cc) were strengthened around the base of the cylinder. As expected, the 1991 900 Supersport also received a new clutch, shared with the 1990–91 851S, with eight steel plates and eight fibre plates rather than the earlier seven of each, while an outer 3.5mm driving plate was used in conjunction with 2.5mm plates. The clutch friction material was modified three times during 1991, in January, March and June, but apart from the carburation and ignition, all other details were identical to the earlier 900 SS; this included the camshafts, valves, crankshaft, gearbox, and 31/62 straight-cut geared primary drive. The 2:1 ratio was an odd choice because there was no hunting tooth effect to spread the load, and these primary drive sets have been known to fail. During 1991 a close-ratio six-speed gearbox suitable for racing became available for all large-crankcase engines. While all 900 Supersports had an oil radiator, the 1991 fitting of this on the front cylinder exhaust rocker cover, just behind the front tyre, was a less satisfactory solution.

Finally the troublesome Weber carburettor was replaced by twin constant-vacuum Mikuni 38 B67 examples, which had initially been tried on the Japanese market 400 Super Sport Junior of 1989 and 1990. While not perfect, they were much better than the Weber. Although the jetting differed for different markets, notably California and Switzerland, it was generally main jet 140, idle jet 42.5, needle jet Y2, starting jet 70, and a 5C19 needle, fourth notch from top. Soon there was trouble with dirt from the front wheel entering the mixture adjustment screw, so these were fitted with small covers from June 1991. With relatively long equal-length inlet manifolds there was still room for a large-capacity air-filter under the reshaped fuel tank. After a brief flirtation with the Marelli Digiplex, ignition returned to the electronic inductive Kokusan of the final F1s. Advance was 6° up to 1,700rpm, and progressively to 32° from 1,700 to 2,600rpm. With the change of ignition there was also a return to the 300-watt alternator.

There were even more significant changes to the chassis. The white-painted chrome-

The 1991 half-faired 900 SS. The engine was all black and the oil radiator was positioned very close to the front wheel. (Australian Motorcycle News)

molybdenum steel frame was similar, but with a steeper steering head angle at 26° 15". Trail was down to 103mm (4 inches) with 25° of steering lock on either side. Not only did the 1991 Supersport steer more quickly, but a new aluminium swing-arm helped reduce the wheelbase to 1,410mm (56½ inches). As with other large-crankcase Ducatis, the swing-arm pivoted on needle roller bearings rather than bronze bushes, still inserted in the crankcases. The footpeg and muffler brackets became bolt-on aluminium pieces, as opposed to the earlier bike's brackets that were part of the frame. Front and rear suspension was also an improvement on the earlier Marzocchis. Shorter inverted 41mm Showa GD 011 forks provided adjustment for spring pre-load (10–25mm), as well as 14 positions for compression and rebound damping. Wheel travel was 120mm (4.7 inches). At the rear there was still the single-shock cantilever rear suspension, also now Showa, a GD

022-007-OX with a piggy-back reservoir, and 65mm (2½ inches) of travel. The 12mm longer shock also contributed to a raised rear end and the quicker steering, effectively 25°.

While the 17-inch Brembo wheels were carried over from the previous 900 Super Sport, the brakes were now standardised with the 851, twin 320 x 5mm stainless steel front discs with Brembo P4 32d callipers on the front. After frame number 001601 these were replaced by the newer gold type with a 34mm leading piston, P4 30/34. The front master cylinder was the PS15 of before, and at the rear was a 245 x 6.4mm disc with a Brembo P2105N calliper. Tyres were Michelin A/M59X.

Huge advances were made in the way that the rest of the motorcycle was put together. Simply by releasing a clip on the front of the tank it could be pivoted to allow easy access to the battery, airbox and fuel pipes. A small decrease in fuel capacity (17.5 as opposed to 18 litres) was a small price to pay for not only the improved function, but also the more attractive shape. All the other bodywork was also new. Only a dual seat was provided, and there were two

Both the fully and half-faired 900 Supersports were produced for 1991. All the frames were white, as were the wheels for that year. (Streetbike)

versions, one fully and one half-faired, both red.

The riding position was also completely revised, the higher handlebars and lower footpegs giving a much less extreme position than the first-generation bevel-gear Super Sports, which were not renowned for their comfort. These new Supersports could be ridden for reasonable distances without crucifying the rider, but the Pantah-derived 904cc motor still was not as smooth as the original and suffered more driveline lash. As before, however, the 900 Supersport generated impressive on-the-road performance by matching low weight with high torque, not big horsepower and technological complexity. Where the 1991 900 Supersport really succeeded was in filling the niche that had been vacant since the demise of its earlier namesake, which the S2, Mike Hailwood Replica and F1 had somehow failed to fill. It was also the first Ducati Super Sport to be produced in larger numbers, 4,305 in 1991 alone (although that figure includes 1992-spec machines built towards the end of the year).

While the 1991 900 Supersport was amazingly well developed, it was continu-ally refined over the next few years, several modifications appearing for 1992 (from September 1991). There was also the limited edition Superlight for that year, which is covered in Chapter 13. Within the engine the flywheel-to-flange fastener screws increased from five to seven. From January 1992 all engines received valve guides of aluminium-bronze rather than the previous cast-iron; engines thus modified received a 'V1' marking on the timing cover side. Clutch modifications continued, and in April 1992 900 engines received a new clutch. The first 3.5mm plate, splined to the clutch housing, was replaced by a 2mm steel plate splined to the clutch drum. This brought the clutch layout to eight 2mm steel driven plates, seven 3mm fibre driving plates, and the curved 1.5mm steel plate that was now inserted after the first driving plate. This clutch would feature on all 900 Supersports until the end of its production in 1997.

For 1992 there was a number a small cosmetic alterations. Still available in both full and half-faired versions, the red 900 SS was supplemented by a black one. The seat unit received a 'SUPERSPORT' decal and also a removable dual seat cowling. There were new decals on the full fairing, and new handgrips; the soft earlier type dated from Paso days and were very prone to wear. Complementing the white frame were the black Brembo wheels that had appeared on the 1991 851 SP3, although black bikes continued with white wheels.

All 1992 Supersports from frame number 003306 had the problematic chain adjuster screws changed from M6 x 70 to a larger M8 x 70, the threaded hole being enlarged to 6.75mm. This affected US models from frame number 002474 to 002505, and 002596 to 002605, and California models from 002578 to 002595. Breakages of seat coverings led to raised frame buffers during April 1992, and that year's production was identical to 1991, at 4,305. In two years the new 900 SS had beaten the total bevel Super Sport figures, and those did not include the Superlights.

It was obvious that Ducati considered the

ABOVE *There were a few small changes to the 900 Supersport in 1992. Together with new graphics and white wheels, there was a rear seat cowling.*

RIGHT *The essence of a Super Sport has always been in how it relates to the rider, and the 1992 900 SS was no different. Although not a racer, a Supersport is still at home on a racing circuit.*

Supersport now very finely honed, as it continued into 1993 with only minor alterations, mainly cosmetic. Within the engine the only change initially was to the alternator, which was now rated at 350 watts, and there was a new engine oil pressure switch. Carburettor icing was still a problem, and in November 1992 a Mikuni carburettor heating kit became available for those engines with an oil-cooler; this ran two pipes from the radiator to the front carburettor float bowl.

During 1993 the M900 Monster went into production, sharing engines and engine numbers with the 900 Supersport. At the same time, in response to a continual problem of cylinder head stud breakage, from July 1993 and engine number 013833 these bolts were increased in diameter from 7.6mm to 8.0mm. There was also a modification to the crankshaft end cap, now with a 0.5mm hole to lubricate the alternator cover bearing.

Alterations to the rest of the motorcycle consisted of a new horn, bronze-painted frame, and new decals, now silver and gold. All Supersports received a 'DESMODUE' decal on the fairing, signifying two-valve. There was a PS16 front master cylinder (with a 16mm piston), and from July 1993, to reduce the stroke of the front brake lever, new front brake callipers to complement this larger master cylinder. These callipers were identified by a blue paint mark and the designations P4 30/34C. Even though the 1993 Superlight had bronze wheels, Supersports continued with the black wheels, and were still available with either a half or full fairing. Supersport production continued almost at previous levels, with 3,853 in 1993.

In an effort to differentiate the 900 from the smaller Supersports, 1994 saw a wider range of modifications and the introduction of two specific US-market 900 Supersports, the 900 CR (Café Racer) and 900 SS SP (Sport Production). Following the failure of the 750 Supersport in the US, the 900 CR took a 900 Supersport engine and mated it with the more basic 750 Supersport running gear with a half fairing. The 900 SP was an amalgam of the Supersport and the Superlight, being basically a fully faired Superlight with a dual seat and lower exhaust pipes. As the SPs were a limited edition version, they are covered with the Superlights in Chapter 13. The details of the 900 CR chassis, with its more basic Showa suspension, are covered with the 1994 750 Supersport in Chapter 12. Engines for the 900 CR and SP differed slightly in their carburation, having Mikuni BDST 38 B73 carburettors; these were identical except for a 37.5 idle jet and 5C 22 needle in the top position. California models received a recycling filter canister.

The only change to the 900 engine for 1994 was to the colour of the engine cases, now painted grey instead of black, but there were more significant changes to the chassis. Not only were the wheels painted bronze to match the frame, but many of the Superlight III features were also now shared with the Supersport, notably the more sophisticated Showa GD 021 fork and stronger aluminium swing-arm. While the fork was of higher specification, it provided less range of adjustment for both compression and rebound damping, four for compression and six for rebound. With the new front fork came a larger-diameter axle and Michelin A/M89 tyres. As with the Superlight, both the clutch and brake master cylinders now had remotely mounted reservoirs. The minor alterations continued with revised seat and helmet locks, a new sidestand, black anodised footpeg brackets and levers, and thinner (4mm) stainless steel brake discs. With the bronze wheels came a bronze instrument panel support. When the 916 went into production in May 1994, all voltage regulators were standardised. Also taking some time to come were offset camshaft keys, now available to fine-tune the valve timing if required; five keys provided advance or retard in a range from 2° to 10°. With US production separated from the regular

A pair of 1995 fully faired 900 Supersports. These were very similar to the 1994 models but for an underslung rear brake calliper and a new dashboard incorporating an oil temperature gauge.

124

Supersport, numbers were 1,685 during 1994, with a further 1,680 going to the United States (both SP and CR).

As usual, 1995 saw a few more minor changes to the 900 Supersport. In November 1994, from engine number 023160 and frame number 016373 there was a new alternator, also standardised with the 916. The timing belt covers and rear sprocket cover were now grey to match the other engine covers, but otherwise engine specifications continued as before. Colour changes extended to a grey side-stand, black horn, and the frame now gold like the 916. Apart from the new colours, other alterations were the rear brake calliper, now mounted underneath the swing-arm, an oil temperature gauge incorporated in the dashboard, and a new windshield. With the new rear brake came a revised rear master cylinder, lever, fluid reservoir location, and brake pads retained by a spring rather than split pins. Dunlop Sportmax tyres were sometimes fitted instead of Michelin. US 900 CRs and SPs also changed for 1995, 900 CRs receiving the Marzocchi fork of the 750 Supersport and the Sachs-Boge shock absorber of the 600 Supersport. After some difficulties in 1994, in the following year production was up to 2,500 900 Supersports and 1,830 US SPs and CRs.

So well developed was the 900 Supersport that for 1996 there were only minor changes. New crankcases had an extra engine bolt near the electric start motor, and the four bolts around the cylinders were lengthened from M8 x 75mm to M8 x 90mm. The bosses on the right crankcase, which had always been present for a possible kickstarter, were finally removed, all engines received a sound-absorbing clutch cover, and the 900 Supersport sometimes sported Pirelli MTR03 tyres. Starting from frame number 021029, a washer was inserted underneath the lower steering head bearing for additional protection. The year 1996 was also very difficult for the company prior to the TPG buy-out in September, and only 1,198 900 SSs, plus 570 for the US, left the factory that year. The next series of alterations was

saved up for 1997, the final year for this series of Supersport.

As sales were now tapering off in relation to the other production lines (Hypersport and Monster), the 900 Supersport specification was upgraded for 1997. In a world of continual change for fashion's sake the Supersport was starting to show its age, so management endeavoured to get a further year of model life by making the Supersport more appealing. There was no longer a Superlight, although there was still a 900 SP for the US, so many of the special Superlight features became standard on the Supersport, notably the carbon-fibre front mudguard, fully floating rear brake, adjustable clutch and brake levers, and braided steel clutch and brake lines (for Europe only). Now only the 900 SP received the 280 x 4.5mm floating cast-iron brake discs, and all 900 Supersports had Michelin HiSport or Pirelli Dragon tyres.

Within the engine, bimetallic exhaust and inlet valves were used for better compatibility with unleaded fuels and to help stabilise valve clearances. All carburettors received the heating kit that had previously been an option, and the oil-cooler radiator was mounted above the front cylinder as it always had been on the Monster. The frame came in for minor revisions to increase the steering angle to 28° on either side. There were also new regulators, made by Shindengen rather than Ducati Energia, and from frame number 025450 there were new brake discs with a revised floating system to smooth the brake operation. New front brake calipers were also fitted from frame number 025220. While looking externally identical they were a new generation internally, with more fluid volume.

The first restyle since 1993 occurred in 1997, with yellow Supersports to complement the red. The revised full fairing incorporated not only integral sound-absorbing panels with new graphics, but also an additional air intake. As always there was the

Half-faired 900 Supersports were offered until 1997, but were not as popular as the fully faired versions. This 1996 Supersport has non-standard carbon-fibre timing belt covers.

The end of a line that started in 1991: the 1997 900 Supersport had a fully floating rear brake and a carbon-fibre front mudguard. The fairing now had air intakes.

option of a half fairing, and with the oil-cooler now mounted higher, the engine looked much tidier than before. There was a new seat, and the black footpeg brackets made a return to anodised aluminium. However, it was still insufficient to halt a downturn in demand, and 900 SS production was reduced even against 1996 levels, at 1,164 900 SSs plus 430 for the United States.

The final Ducatis with the older Cagiva-style graphics were 200 red and 200 yellow 900 CRs for the United States, completed early in 1998. These were the final Ducatis with the older-style graphics, and they had 1998-specification engines (new pistons and

cylinders), but with the oil-cooler mounted underneath the front cylinder.

As expected after seven years, the 1997 Supersport was a thoroughly refined and well-developed motorcycle, but it now looked out of date with the square head-light and basic 1991 styling. Moreover, after having the 90° V-twin market all to itself for so long, the 900 SS was now facing competition from the Japanese, but even so the Supersport could hold its own. It may have suffered in the power department, but the all-round package of balanced rideabil-ity and handling meant that it was still a force to be reckoned with. A replacement was needed, but it would be well into 1998 before a new Supersport would be avail-able. In the meantime the final series, the 900 SS FE, was released, but as it was a limited edition it is covered in Chapter 13.

12

Smaller brothers

Smaller Supersports followed on in the wake of the 900. Soon after the release of the revised 1991 Supersport, there was a similar 750 Supersport to supersede the earlier unremarkable 750 Sport. It still used the smaller crankcase five-speed Pantah engine, now without an oil-cooler, but otherwise the engine was much as before, with the same camshafts and the same 36/71 primary drive ratio. Soon after the 750 came a 400 and 350, primarily for the Japanese and domestic Italian markets. These were not the first 400 Supersports, however; during 1989 a special Japanese-market 400 Super Sport Junior, derived from the 750 Sport, had been produced.

While this 1989 400 Super Sport Junior certainly had not set the world alight with its performance, it was an interesting motorcycle from several standpoints. The first Ducati to use twin Mikuni CV carburettors, it was

A 400 SS Junior of 1991. The 350 and 400 Supersports only existed to circumvent insurance regulations and were primarily for the Japanese and Italian markets. Like all Supersports they came in both fully and half-faired versions. (Australian Motorcycle News)

also a precursor of the 1991 Supersport with its white frame and 851-style twin exhausts. Wheels were the composite Marvic 16-inch that had featured on the 1988 851 Strada, complete with floating cast-iron brake discs, twin 280mm on the front and 260mm at the rear. With 300 built in 1989, plus a further 300 in 1990, the success of this model in Japan paved the way for further 400s. However, putting a small engine in essentially a 750 chassis was never going to be the recipe for success.

The 1991 smaller Supersports were the 750, 400 SS Junior, and 350 Sport. Many more 750s were made, 1,872 as against 500, but these figures also include 1992 model year bikes produced after September. All were red, with white wheels and frame, and had a quite basic specification and chassis to keep prices reasonable. Most were fitted with half fairings, and all had non-adjustable 41mm Showa GD031 front suspension. The 350 Sport and 750 SS shared their Showa GD022 shock absorber with the larger 900 Supersport, but for some reason the 400 SS Junior had a Marzocchi PBS1R shock absorber. Both the 350 and 400 offered less front fork travel than the 750, at 103mm. All small Supersports had aluminium swing-arms for 1991, and a single 320mm stainless-steel front disc brake with a Brembo P4 30/34 calliper with a PS13 master cylinder. The rear rim width was less than for the 900, at 4.50 x 17 inches, and tyres varied from model to model: the 400 SS Junior and 750 SS had Michelin A/M59X, while the 350 received Dunlop Sportmax, probably to test them on the local market before using them on more models during the next year.

Engines were black, the 350s and 400s having the six-speed gearbox and 34/77 primary gears of the earlier 350 and 400 F3. Valve sizes for both the little Super Sports were 33.5 and 30.5mm, the 350 receiving slightly smaller-diameter exhaust pipes (100mm against 110mm). Both the 350 and 400 had a two-into-one exhaust system with the muffler on the right side, not the left as in the earlier F1 and F3. For 1991 (350, 400 and 750) the smaller dry clutch carried over from the 750 Sport (seven steel and seven fibre plates), but was of two possible types; if a 3.5mm outer plate was used, all the other plates were 2.5mm, and with a 2.75mm outer plate the other discs were 2.6mm. From September 1991 a 900-style oil-cooler kit became available for the 750 Supersport.

In 1992 the 350 Sport was re-named the 350 Supersport Junior, but otherwise there were few changes apart from the adoption of the wet clutch of the 750 SS, which affected bikes from engine number 000202 (350) and 000008 (400). The 350 and 400 were the only red Supersports to continue with white wheels, and production was well up on the previous year, at 1,051 units.

There were a few more alterations to the 750 SS for 1992 (from engine number 001275). Within the engine there was now a hydraulically operated wet clutch with eight 1.5mm steel driven plates, eight fibre 2.5mm driving plates, and one outside 3.5mm driving plate. Complementing the new clutch were straight-cut primary gears with the 31/62 (2:1) ratio of the 900. The oil-cooler that had become an option late in 1991 was now a standard fitting. As with the 900, the 1992 engines (from January) received aluminium-bronze valve guides instead of cast iron. Production of the 750 matched the level set in 1991, again with 1,872 manufactured.

In line with the 900, the 750 Supersports, from frame number 001210, were fitted with the stronger chain adjusters (M8 x 70 bolts). Also for 1992, the 750 SS had black wheels and Dunlop Sportmax tyres, which were also shared with the 350 and 400. In April 1992 the 350, 400 and 750 were fitted with raised seat buffers to prevent interference and chafing on the bodywork. Fully faired 750s were also available in addition to half-faired, with the option of black (with black wheels) as an alternative to red. As the single front disc was marginal on the 750, a twin-disc kit was offered as a factory option in June 1992, but would still not appear as standard for more than a year.

The white-painted frame continued for 1992, but the 750 Supersport now had a wet clutch and an oil-cooler. (Two Wheels)

A 1992 half-faired 750 Supersport. Unlike the 900, the 750 did not receive a seat cowling. (Two Wheels)

Continual upgrading of the smaller Supersports continued as the entire range was developed, and for 1993 there were the bronze frame and new decals that typified all of that year's Ducatis. The biggest change was to the swing-arm, the previous aluminium being replaced by one of steel. With the new swing-arm there were also new footpegs and a rear brake master cylinder similar to the 900. Now the 350, 400 and 750 Supersports received black wheels, but only 900s had the solo seat cowling. All the engine specifications were carried through but for the carburettor jetting for the 400 Supersport; after engine number 000802 there was modified jetting, a 122.5 main jet and 5CH 07 needle jet, with the needle now in the third position. Production was significantly increased for 1993, with 2,352 750s and 950 350/400s built.

There was much more in store for the smaller Supersports in 1994, buoyed by the addition of a 600. The 350 was discontinued, and in its place there were now two versions of the 400, one 27bhp version for Europe (specifically Germany), and a 42bhp

version for Japan and Italy. From the 400 grew a 600 Supersport, also in two versions, 33 and 53bhp. While the 400, now with a revised ignition advance, continued with the six-speed gearbox as before, the 600 had five speeds like the 750. Both the 400 and 600 received a new set of primary gears (32/73) and continued with the wet clutch from the 750 Supersport. The last 600 Ducati had been the 600 SL Pantah of 1984, and there were many similarities between the two even though they were ten years apart. They shared the same bore and stroke (80 x 58mm), but surprisingly the cylinder heads for the 600 SS were from the 400, still with the small 33.5 and 30.5mm valves (the earlier 600 SL had 37.5 and 33.5mm valves). Engines for 1994 featured grey side covers, and the 600 joined the 400 by having a two-into-one exhaust system. For all Mikuni-carburated bikes without an oil-cooler there was a special carburettor heating kit available from June 1994. The 600 proved to be an

Introduced in 1994, the 600 Supersport recalled the days of the 600SL Pantah of the early 1980s. The 600 Supersport was also available with a full fairing and remained largely unchanged through to this 1996 version.

immediate success, with 2,355 produced in 1994.

With only 150 400 Supersports manufactured in 1994, they shared with the 750 Super Sport the 41mm Showa forks (with 120mm of travel) and rear shock absorber. The 600 featured new Marzocchi 40mm USD/E forks and a Sachs-Boge shock, and all models now had the larger-diameter front axle. Wheels for 1994 were bronze for all Super Sports, and there was a new side-stand and black anodised footpeg brackets and levers. Both the 600 and the final 400s were also offered with either full or half fairings, and the 600 received revised helmet fasteners and seat location.

It had been intended to discontinue the 400 Supersport, so to keep uniformity within the range the clutch and primary gears of the 750 and 900 SS were also fitted to 600s. From engine number 001853 the primary ratio was now 31/62 (2.00:1) with a 15/41 final drive ratio, up from 32/73 (2.28:1) with 15/36 rear sprockets.

With the introduction of the 600 SS, the 750 was upgraded slightly to place it apart from the newer model. In 1994 the production of the 750 was also much less than the 600, at only 1,008 units. The 750 also received all the 1994 changes to engine colours and footpegs, but the most significant inclusion was a standard front 280mm dual disc that had been an option for the previous year. Unlike the 600, the 750 continued with Showa suspension during 1994, and was complemented by a 900 CR for the United States. To cater for a climate where 'bigger is better', the 750 Supersport was no longer offered in the US, and in its place was the 900 CR, a 900 Supersport in the 750 chassis. Only available with a half fairing, this Ducati for the budget-conscious still used non-adjustable Showa suspension, a 4.5 x 17-inch rear wheel, Dunlop Sportmax tyres, and a steel swing-arm.

As more resources were put into the

For 1997 the 750 Supersport was also available in yellow. The fairing had additional air intakes, and there were new graphics and a rear seat cowling; dual front discs had become standard in 1994.

134

Monster and Hypersport lines, the Supersport range was rationalised for 1995. It was no surprise to see the demise of the underpowered 400, the 600 remaining as the smallest Ducati. All the front suspension for the 600, 750 and 900 CR was standardised to 40mm Marzocchi, 750 Super Sports from frame number 007707 having the Marzocchis. While the 600 and 900 CR had the Sachs-Boge rear shock absorber, the 750 still used the Showa GD 022. The 600 Super Sport Marzocchi forks differed in that the right fork leg was now without a brake calliper attachment. Colour changes mirrored those of the 900 Super Sport: 916-style gold frame, black horn, and grey timing belt covers, rear sprocket cover and sidestand. The 1995 600 Supersports from engine number 05025 and frame number 002287 had a modified vertical cylinder and piston assembly to overcome reliability problems. Also, 600 Supersports from frame number 002601 to 002900, and 750 Supersports from frame number 008201 to 008900, had problems with interference between the alternator rotor and stator, caused by deformation of the stator due to interference with the bushes. After a slight lull in 1994, production of the 750 was healthy once again with 1,550 constructed, although 600 Supersport production was down considerably to 737.

There were very few changes for 1996 except for a return to limited production of 200 of the 400 Supersport for the local market. In October 1995, starting from frame number 009401 for the 750 Supersport and 002853 for the 600 Supersport, a washer was inserted beneath the lower steering head bearing. Both the 600 and 750 received sound-deadening panels, and the 600 a stainless-steel exhaust system. That year was a difficult one for the factory, and only 60 750 Supersports and 463 600 Supersports were produced. As with the 900, most alterations would be saved for the 1997 model year.

In a choice of red or yellow, and fully or half-faired, Ducati was aiming to get the most from the Supersport as it neared the end of its production run. As for the 900, there was a new fairing with an air intake, new graphics, bimetallic inlet and exhaust valves, a 28° steering angle, carburettor heating kit, and anodised aluminium foot-peg brackets. The oil-cooler on the 750 Supersport was now mounted above the front cylinder away from the stones flicked by the front wheel. During 1997 the Ducati Energia regulators were replaced by Shindengen and there were new brake callipers and front brake discs with a different spring loading system. The revised callipers were from chassis number 003598 on the 600 SS, and 010113 on the 750 SS. New discs were fitted from 400 SS 001956, 600 SS 003754 and 750 SS 010189. There was yet another change to the pistons and cylinders for the 600 Supersport, with new piston assemblies from chassis number 003752 (engine number 012938). With the company's production difficulties behind them following the TPG buy-out of September 1996, 1,146 750s and 801 600s were built during 1997. There were also another 200 of the 400 Supersport for the Italian market.

Although production of the smaller Supersports was discontinued for 1998, later in that year there would be a new 750 Supersport patterned on the revised 900. With fuel injection, other features that had always characterised the 750 Supersport would be retained, including non-adjustable 43mm Showa forks and a steel swing-arm. Planned production was for 1,145 in 1998, with the possibility of a 600 version to follow.

Overshadowed by the 900, the smaller Supersports have always had a place in Ducati's recent line-up, serving their purpose as an entry-level sporting Ducati and a chance to experience the mystique at a reasonable price. While the 400s and the 33bhp 600s really only existed to circumvent insurance anomalies, the other small-crankcase Supersports gave away little to their larger siblings other than horsepower, brakes, and suspension sophistication. Consequently they offered all the traditional Supersport appeal at a lesser price. Unfortunately they have suffered through being the supporting act rather than the main event.

CHAPTER 13

Superlight: limited edition Supersport

In late September 1991 Cagiva held a lavish dealer conference in Rome to announce the 1992 motorcycle range. While the restyled 888 SP4 was expected to steal the limelight, the surprise release was a limited edition 900 Supersport, called the Superlight. Taking the already light Supersport and adding carbon-fibre mudguards, lightweight Marvic composite wheels with cast-iron discs, a solo seat and upswept exhaust pipes, an alluring motorcycle was created. This was the Super Sport concept taken to its zenith.

Unlike other limited edition Ducatis, however, the Superlight used the standard 900 Super Sport engine, and ultimately this would be its downfall. Although it remained in production for five years, the Superlight was not as successful as it probably should have been. As well as being limited by only a solo seat, what the Superlight really needed to set it apart from the regular Supersport was more horsepower. As it was it failed to become the successor to the first 750 Super Sport, or even the 750 Monjtuich, Laguna Seca or Santa Monica. The other problem with the Superlight was that too many were built for it to be a real limited edition, and after the first series it suffered from an identity crisis when it lost most of the special lightweight parts. Ducati could be criticised for abusing the limited edition, a fact acknowledged by Ing. Massimo Bordi when I discussed the future of the Superlight with him in 1998.

Like so many prototypes, the Superlight displayed to dealers was noticeably different from the eventual production version. Hastily conceived out of a regular 1992 900 Supersport, the only differences were the 17-inch Marvic composite wheels, solo seat and upswept exhaust with crude aluminium brackets. While this prototype had no white number plate on the seat, one appeared when it was used for the publicity brochure. By now it had a neater exhaust bracket, but still not the vented clutch or cast-iron disc rotors. When it went into production the Superlight had both the vented clutch and 320 x 4.5mm floating cast-iron front disc rotors, adding to its appeal. The mufflers (from the 888 SP4) were a larger diameter that standard, and stepped down to fit the standard 900 SS collector. Of all the Superlights, the 1992 version most effectively epitomised the concept of minimum weight, later versions being compromised by the use of standard wheels.

Setting the Superlight apart from its stable mate was a numbered plaque on the top triple clamp. Apart from the Marvic wheels (in the same 3.50 x 17 and 5.50 x 17-inch sizes) the rolling chassis was unchanged. There were some troubles with the wheels on several 1992 Superlights; in frame numbers 004456 to 004750 and 004951 to 005306 there was a loosening of the rear wheel hub retaining screws, and a modification provided six new screws. Tyres for 1992 were Michelin A/M89X.

The first Superlight of 1992 was also produced in the most numbers. One of the most desirable of modern Ducatis, it featured Marvic composite wheels.

Although the claimed weight was 7 kilograms less than the regular 900 Super Sport, this was probably slightly optimistic, and the Superlight was a similar on-the-road performer. How limited edition was that first Superlight? Not very, as 1,317 were built. They were red for Europe and yellow for the United States, with numbers well above other limited edition Ducatis. US Superlights used a separate number sequence.

Significant changes appeared on the Superlight for 1993, not least an increase in weight through the use of regular Brembo wheels. While the Super Sport had black wheels for this year, the Superlight shared its bronze wheels and Michelin TX11/23 tyres with the 888 SP5, as well as a fully floating rear brake linkage. Like the SP5 this was initially via a carbon-fibre tie-rod, but following failures this was soon changed to an aluminium one. Also absent for 1993 was the vented clutch cover, and while the brochures indicated that Superlights would receive floating cast-iron

front discs, all production 1993 Superlights had the regular Supersport stainless-steel rotors. They still received the rectangular numbered plaque, however, now with a 'Superlight II' designation.

Small styling changes appeared on the Superlight II. In line with other 1993 bikes the frames were painted bronze, with new gold and silver decals. The Superlight now had a large '1' in the white plate on the seat, and this would continue through to the Superlight V. With the entire chassis being shared with the 900 Supersport, to many it seemed that the Superlight II offered nothing over a standard 900 Supersport except a numbered plaque and carbon-fibre front guard. On top of that it was more expensive. Even so, 861 were manufactured in 1993.

Fortunately some amendments were made for the Superlight III of 1994. Most were now in the yellow that had appeared on the first US Superlights of 1992, although red was still available. All the engine and chassis specifications continued unchanged from the 900 Supersport of 1994, but upgraded Showa GD 021 forks, similar to those of the earlier 888 SP5, were used on the front, although the rear Showa GD 022 was unchanged. The Superlight also received a stronger aluminium swing-arm, and while these were an advance over the earlier 900 Superlight, they too were shared with the regular bike. Other changes that appeared on all 1994 bikes were the grey engine covers, new sidestand, black footpeg brackets and levers, larger-diameter front wheel axle, Michelin A/M89X tyres, new seat and helmet locking system, and remote reservoirs for the brake and clutch master cylinders. While it was undeniably an improvement over 1993, all that differentiated the Superlight III from the Supersport was a solo seat, carbon-fibre clutch cover and mudguards, a fully floating rear disc, and a return to the floating cast-iron front discs. Of course there was also the number on the top triple clamp with production down slightly from the previous year, at 719. Still, it was barely a true limited edition.

After the yellow Superlight of 1992, there were no more Superlights for the United States, but a specific 900 SS SP (Sport Production) was created to supplement the more basic 900 CR (Café Racer) for 1994. The Sport Production was not a real SP in the true sense of the word. Sport Production

Ducatis had originated in 1989 as special performance racing versions of the 851 for the Italian Sport Production racing series. As the 900 SP offered no performance increase, it was more of a marketing ploy following on from the success of the real 851, 888 and 916 SPs. If the 900 SP had been sold elsewhere it may have contributed to the Superlight having a longer production run, since it was in effect a dual-seat Superlight. The SPs were red only, and like all Superlights only came with a full fairing. They also came with a numbered plaque, with 'Supersport SP', and a different sequence from the Superlight. Apart from the dual seat and lower mufflers, Supersport SPs shared all the refinements of the Superlight III, with carbon-fibre clutch cover and front and rear mudguards, fully floating rear disc brake, and floating cast-iron front disc rotors. Although it was claimed to be a limited production bike, SP numbers were about half of the total 1,680

After 1992 there were no more Superlights for the United States; they received the SS Sport Production instead. Essentially a Superlight with a dual seat, this is a 1996 900 SS SP.

All Superlights received a numbered plaque on the top triple clamp. The Superlight IV was from 1995, and most were yellow.

900 Supersports shipped to the United States during 1994.

There were only a few cosmetic alterations for 1995, most notably a grey side-stand, timing belt covers and rear sprocket cover. The frame colour was now 916 gold, and like the other Supersports there was a new windshield. Superlight IVs received a revised seating support, with two brackets and two rubber pads. Looking very similar to the Superlight III, the oil temperature gauge on the dashboard was the main give-away, together with the usual 'Superlight IV' numbered plaque. As with the previous year, most of the 578 Superlight IVs were in yellow.

The success of the 900 SS SP in the United States during 1994 ensured its continuation, with even more being produced, around 850 for 1995. Basically it was also identical to the earlier version, but with the usual changes that appeared on the Superlight IV that year. Even though the Superlight was selling slowly, with less production every year, the Superlight V was offered for 1996. However, production was a long way from the halcyon days of 1992 with only 300 constructed. More successful was the SP for the United States. Virtually unchanged, SPs were fitted with Dunlop Sportmax radial tyres, sound-deadening fairings, and continued with the numbered plaque.

By 1997 the Superlight's problem was that it did not offer much over the regular Supersport to justify its higher price tag. On top of that there was the inflexibility of a solo seat, although that may have been overcome if, like the SP versions of the 851, 888, and 916, the Superlight had provided more performance. With no extra power, only marginally better braking, and not even the prospect of being rare and valuable, the days of the Superlight were numbered. Although not available as a 1997 model, the 900 SS SP continued for the United States.

As the regular 1997 900 SS incorporated most of the previous Superlight features, the SP and SS were now very similar. Distinguished only by the numbered plaque, floating cast-iron discs and carbon-fibre rear mudguard and clutch cover, the SP also did not receive the braided steel brake lines of the regular Supersport, these not being legal in the United States.

With the release of the new fuel-injected Supersport on the horizon, one final Superlight series of the carburetted model was produced before production of the new model commenced. Harking back to the

One last Superlight series was constructed before the fuel-injected Supersport appeared. This is 900 SS Final Edition No 001 on the Futa Pass near Bologna in January 1998. Sprinkled with carbon-fibre, the FE was a Supersport for the traditionalist.

days of the silver and blue 900 Super Sports, the 900 FE (Final Edition) had silver bodywork with new graphics, accentuated by black wheels. There were two versions, one for Europe and one for the United States. The 500 European FEs were constructed in late 1997 and used 1997-specification engines with silver engine covers and external cylinder oil lines. They also had a carbon-fibre clutch cover and steel brake lines. The 300 US 900 FEs were produced in January 1998 and used 1998-specification engines (shared with the Monster 900S) with grey engine covers and clutch cover. The new Tecnol cylinders were neater looking as the oil lines were now incorporated internally. As usual for the United States, these bikes had rubber brake lines. Much of the rest of the FE specifica-

tion was as for the earlier Superlight, with a solo seat, upswept Termignoni exhausts, cast-iron floating front brake discs, and carbon-fibre mudguards. Carbon-fibre also extended to the chainguard and simplified dashboard (without a battery warning light). With all 800 carrying a numbered plaque, these final classic carburetted Supersports were destined to become collectors' items.

Yet all good things must come to an end, and by 1998 the design was in need of updating. Other Ducatis in the line-up now had more sophisticated brakes and suspension, and the square headlight was a remnant of the 750 F1. This is where Pierre Terblanche stepped in, the replacement 900 Supersport being displayed at Milan in September 1997.

14

The Supersport today and tomorrow

Although there had been talk of a replacement Supersport for several years, financial problems saw the project continually delayed. During 1995–96 Ducati was having enough difficulty in supplying existing models, let alone creating new ones. The TPG buy-out of September 1996 immediately produced a climate that allowed a new Supersport to proceed. However, it was not until 15 December 1996 that the project really got under way when Massimo Bordi approached Pierre Terblanche and asked him to co-ordinate the design programme. Terblanche, well known to Ducati for the magnificent Supermono racing single of 1992, was at that stage working in nearby San Marino at the Cagiva Research Centre with Massimo Tamburini. Sketches started immediately, and Terblanche resigned from CRC on 19 December to concentrate fully on the new Supersport.

Pierre Terblanche is a designer with a genuine interest in preserving the history of Ducati. Since his boyhood days in South Africa he has been a Ducati enthusiast and proudly displays a large photo of himself with a 1973 750 Sport in his studio. 'It is my dream to replicate those bikes,' he says. 'I would like to see the engines more attractive so as to be part of the overall aesthetic concept as they were with the older bikes. There were some absolute styling miracles in the '70s, particularly the NCR racing bikes. My view of the Super Sport of the future is to somehow revive the great bikes of the past – bikes like the 750 SS and the Mike Hailwood Replica.'

Bordi's brief to Terblanche was quite specific, with immediate implementation an important element. 'The original idea was that we had to take a standard carry-over frame, existing taillight, with the bottom of the tank also a carry-over part. This was important because the tooling for a steel fuel tank is one of the most expensive components when creating a new model. Basically I wasn't allowed to change too much from the Supersport concept because the Supersport customer is very traditional. The bike still had to be comfortable, obviously not touring comfortable but more so than a Hypersports, a two-seater, and with much the same type of riding position as before. This was something I modified. I decided that as we had the ST2 we could go for a slightly more sporting riding position. From research we found that we could position the handlebars down and back slightly. They've been pulled back about 15mm so they're closer to the rider but are still above the triple clamps. It's a little bit more comfortable I think for the average rider. The brief was also to keep it simple, hence we have not gone for water-cooling.

'The frame had to be almost exactly the same as before. While it may look the same, the rear section is completely new and the steering head angle is steepened by 1 degree. That has helped enormously. The footpeg

New-generation forks, wheels and brakes were a feature of the new Supersport.

position is also similar to before so the riding position is slightly more comfortable than the 916. The exhaust we couldn't change, but we were able to narrow some frame tubes. Although we still needed to maintain the cantilever rear suspension, more rear wheel travel means this works much better. The rear number plate is from the ST2, one of the ST2's nicest features. Obviously with a very short lead time to production we tried to use as many components as we could from existing models, but only in those areas where I felt they were good enough to be carried over. We didn't choose anything on the bike that I didn't think was the right quality. The one thing that has changed is that we have now fitted 916 instruments, with new graphics. On the original prototype they were 900 SS. Personally I still like the old ones, the Veglia Borletti. They're very good quality but they are maybe too old now for some people.'

Other shared components were the front forks and brakes, from the ST2. The 43mm Showa forks were new-generation, as were the Brembo brakes. The calliper mounts were wider apart to improve rigidity, and the callipers different internally with greater fluid capacity. Both the clutch and front brake master cylinders were also a new generation, with revised lever ratios. The Brembo front wheel was 916, and the rear ST2. To maintain a uniformity within the range the footpegs and controls were also from the 916. The bike was slightly heavier than before, at 186kg, because of the stronger front forks and larger silencers.

'Keeping the weight down is becoming increasingly difficult,' says Terblanche. 'Of course it is possible with an unlimited budget but really not practical. We don't think the use of titanium exhausts like the Japanese is practical because of the replacement cost if they get damaged. We also want to keep our customers happy.

'The first 19 or 20 sketches were completed the day before Christmas 1996,' he continues. 'The difficulty was that Ducati don't really have any design facilities – all the bikes have previously been done outside, either at Varese, Galluzzi at Cagiva Morizone, or Tamburini at CRC. The

One of the prototypes for the 1998 900 Supersport. More than 30,000 kilometres were put on these mules on mountain roads around Bologna during testing.

people I knew were in the UK so I phoned Futura Design, a modelling company in Birmingham, and asked if they could do us a big favour by giving us a hand with the bike. [Futura have done a lot of work for Rolls-Royce and Isuzu.]

'So from 9 January to 3 April 1997 I worked at Futura on clay mock-ups. We got a Supersport from the British importer, changed the whole back of the frame, used new footpeg mounts, cut the tank away except for its base, and bolted the bike down on a modelling plate. It was all done by hand from sketches and the bike came back as it is now. It was the quickest I have ever done.'

It needed to be done quickly as the Supersport would be the only major new Ducati for 1998. 'What we need to do now is move on technology wise and start doing everything with three-dimensional computers to speed up development time. In the future we will use mathematical surfaces and it is an area where bikes are lagging behind cars. It can be very slow the old-fashioned way. This bike, from the first sketch on paper through to the production bike, took about 15 months using some mathematical surfaces. By Ducati standards that is pretty quick. It has also been a very difficult project. A full Hypersports bike is easier to design in many ways because there are fewer road bike compromises. With a low front and high rear it is much easier to get a bike to look purposeful and complete. Here we have a road bike rather than a racer, and to get this to look sporting and co-ordinated is not so easy. Also I have tried to maintain similar lines between the creases in the tank and seat, much as I did with the Supermono, but with steel instead of carbon-fibre this is more difficult. The bike is not at its best viewed from underneath as it was on display in the motorcycle shows.'

There were a number of significant alterations to the engine, notably the use of

Although sharing the basic frame with the earlier Supersport, Terblanche's design was refreshingly new while still maintaining its traditional appeal.

Weber Marelli electronic fuel injection. To complement the injection there are new camshafts (with new valve timing – see Appendix), the engine running more cleanly, and with an increase of about 5bhp, under 3,000rpm. Ducati now have a sophisticated computer program to develop new camshafts and this has contributed to the smoother running. Unlike aftermarket or racing camshafts, emission and noise levels are a major consideration with a production

bike. The new camshafts and injection system meant that there was no need for a high-inertia flywheel, and a lighter one could be used. As Terblanche says, 'This bike still has about 30bhp more than most people can handle. Ducatis have always offered a balance between power and on-the-road performance and this Supersport is no different.'

The Weber Marelli fuel injection ECU, code-named the '1.5', was the third genera-

tion to be used by Ducati. The first generation 'P8' of the 851 of 1988 was originally intended for cars with multi-point injection, and still used on those engines with twin injectors per cylinder (916 SPS) ten years later. In 1995 there was a second-generation ECU, the '1.6', specifically designed for single-point injection, and this was used on engines with single injectors. It had fewer channels and was smaller and cheaper than the P8. Finally, there was the '1.5', the first

Marelli processor designed for a motorcycle application. Not only was it cheaper and smaller again, but it could also be adapted for multi-point and be used for twin injectors, although the Supersport only used a single injector per cylinder. Incorporating the absolute air pressure sensor inside the ECU, it promised better reliability, eventually finding its way to the entire Ducati line-up. With the injection system came a new 10-litre airbox.

Other engine changes for 1998 were new cylinders (Tecnol), pistons (Asso), and piston rings (NPR) in place of the previous Mondial items. The redesigned cylinders incorporated the oil return inside, making external oil lines unnecessary. There were also new intake manifolds and a new 520-watt alternator. Finally the troublesome 31/62 primary drive became the 32/59 (1.84:1) of the ST2 and 916 SPS. While many observers expected the new Supersport to grow in size to 944cc like the ST2, marginal cooling of the oil/air-cooled rear cylinder forbade this, and there was new ducting to the rear cylinder. For those wishing for more displacement and horse-power, Ducati Performance was established in 1997 as a 50/50 joint venture with Gia.Ca.Moto in Bologna. A full range of performance-enhancing options was available for those wishing to either customise or hot-rod their Supersport.

Styling is one thing, but the soul of the Supersport is in the way it relates to the rider. It has always been a tribute to Ducati's development department that just about every Ducati has been one that communicates directly with the rider. Ing. Andrea Forni has been responsible for the development of all new motorcycles since 1988, and is an expert rider himself. The nearby Apennines have always been an ideal testing ground and Forni is particularly enthusiastic about the latest Supersport. 'I have done 10,000 kilometres on mountain roads and this new bike is the best handling in the range. On a par with the 748 and better than the 916.

'We started with three mules, basically fuel-injected 1997 Supersports, and progressed from there. Several camshaft profiles were tested, as well as injection programs, but while we started with the old-style forks we worked hard on the chassis to bring it more up to date.' A total of 30,000 kilometres was racked up on various prototypes before the frame specifications were finalised.

'We steepened the steering head to 24° and tested front fork steering offset between 35mm and 32.5mm before settling on 30mm,' says Forni.

'For 90% of road use we believe that the cantilever rear suspension is a good compromise. It is lighter and simpler and with rising rates generally becoming more linear, linkage suspension is not so critical on a sports bike. Of course with a tourer carrying luggage it is different, and also for racing when you need to be able to fine-tune the suspension. In these cases a linkage is useful.'

The stroke on the Showa GD132-007-00 shock absorber was also increased to 71mm (up from 65mm), and new damping was used in the 43mm Showa forks, the improvement being particularly noticeable during hard braking on a bumpy surface. While the weight distribution was unchanged, the riding position was now considerably more sporting.

Says Forni, 'While the comfort may be a little bit lower, the riding position is now very good for the true sporting rider, and closer to the 916.

'We have designed this bike for the typical sportbike rider who rides mainly on the road. The emphasis is still on simplicity and lightness and on a mountain road the new Supersport is unequalled. The power is good for the road with strong low and mid-range power, and this bike probably sets a new parameter for handling, in this case due to the new front suspension set-up and steering geometry.'

Unlike the 1997 Supersports, the 1998 versions were two-seater only, with no rear seat cowling. Later there will be a single-seat version.

The frontal aspect of the 1998 900 Supersport was completely new, and the riding position more sporty than before.

Symbols of the new era: the new Supersport and the ST2 mural at the factory in Bologna.

'We plan to do a Superlight version with a totally redesigned seat unit,' says Pierre Terblanche. 'The choice was made to keep it what it is, either a two-seater or single-seater, nothing in between that does neither as well.'

With production beginning in March 1998, the fuel-injected Supersport became available in Europe during May, and in the United States in July. Production was scheduled for 4,585 units during the year.

While the Supersport is primarily sold as a street bike, racing has always been associated with Ducati and the 1998 Supersport took to the Italian circuits in the 'Supersport Cup'. Prepared by *Techna Racing* in Rome, these specially prepared solo-seat Supersports were allocated by lot over a six-race series, similar to the arrangement for the 'Ducati Monster Cup' during 1997.

By combining innovative styling, electronic fuel injection and modern running gear with the traditional desmodromic two-valve twin-cylinder engine, trellis frame and cantilever rear suspension, Ducati have united the best of both worlds with the Supersport. While undoubtedly a motorcycle to take the Supersport concept into the next century, Ducati have managed to retain the soul that made the Super Sport a classic back in 1974.

Specifications of Ducati Super Sports, 1974–1998

Model	750 SS	750 SS	900 SS	750 SS
Year	1974	1975–77	1975–76	1978–79
Bore (mm)	80	80	86	80
Stroke (mm)	74.4	74.4	74.4	74.4
Capacity (cc)	748	748	864	748
Compression ratio	9.5:1	9.65:1	9.5:1	9.65:1
Max rpm	8500	8800	7900	8800
Valve timing inlet (open/close)	63° btdc 83° abdc	63° btdc 83° abdc	63° btdc 83° abdc	63° btdc 83° abdc
Valve timing exhaust (open/close)	80° bbdc 58° atdc	80° bbdc 58° atdc	80° bbdc 58° atdc	80° bbdc 58° atdc
Carburation	Dell'Orto PHM40A	Dell'Orto PHM40A/ PHF32A	Dell'Orto PHM40A/ PHF32A	Dell'Orto PHF32A
Front tyre	3.50V18	3.50V18	3.50V18	3.50V18
Rear tyre	3.50V18	4.25V18	4.25V18	4.25V18
Front brake (mm)	278 twin disc	280 twin disc	280 twin disc	280 twin disc
Rear brake (mm)	230 disc	229 disc	229 disc	229 disc
Wheelbase (mm)	1530	1500	1500	1500
Seat height (mm)	700	770	770	770
Length (mm)	2230	2220	2220	2220
Width (mm)	660	675	675	675
Weight (kg)	180	187	188	187

Model	900 SS	900 SSD	900 MHR	900 SS
Year	1977–80	1979–81	1979–80	1981–82
Bore (mm)	86	86	86	86
Stroke (mm)	74.4	74.4	74.4	74.4
Capacity (cc)	864	864	864	864
Compression ratio	9.5:1	9.5:1	9.5:1	9.3:1
Max rpm	7900	7800	7900	7800
Valve timing inlet (open/close)	63° btdc 83° abdc	63° btdc 83° abdc	63° btdc 83° abdc	63° btdc 83° abdc
Valve timing exhaust (open/close)	80° bbdc 58° atdc	80° bbdc 58° atdc	80° bbdc 58° atdc	80° bbdc 58° atdc
Carburation	Dell'Orto PHM40A/ PHF32A/C	Dell'Orto PHF32C	Dell'Orto PHM40A	Dell'Orto PHM40A/ PHF32A
Front tyre	3.50V18	3.50V18	100/90V18	3.50V18
Rear tyre	4.25V18	120/90V18	110/90V18	4.25/85V18
Front brake (mm)	280 twin disc	280 twin disc	280 twin disc	280 twin disc
Rear brake (mm)	229 disc	280 disc	280 disc	280 disc
Wheelbase (mm)	1500	1550	1510	1500
Seat height (mm)	770	740	800	840
Length (mm)	2220	2260	2200	2210
Width (mm)	675	700	700	690
Weight (kg)	188	216	205	205

Model	900 MHR	900 S2	900 MHR	1000 S2
Year	1981–82	1982–84	1983–84	1984–85
Bore (mm)	86	86	86	88
Stroke (mm)	74.4	74.4	74.4	80
Capacity (cc)	864	864	864	973
Compression ratio	9.3:1	9.3:1	9.3:1	9.3:1
Max rpm	7900	7800	7800	7500
Valve timing inlet (open/close)	63° btdc 83° abdc	63° btdc 83° abdc	63° btdc 83° abdc	63° btdc 83° abdc
Valve timing exhaust (open/close)	80° bbdc 58° atdc	80° bbdc 58° atdc	80° bbdc 58° atdc	80° bbdc 58° atdc
Carburation	Dell'Orto PHM40A	Dell'Orto PHM40B/ PHF32A	Dell'Orto PHM40B	Dell'Orto PHM40B
Front tyre	3.50V18	100/90V18	100/90V18	100/90V18
Rear tyre	4.25/85V18	110/90V18	120/90V18	130/90V18
Front brake (mm)	280 twin disc	280 twin disc	280 twin disc	280 twin disc
Rear brake (mm)	280 disc	280 disc	280 disc	280 disc
Wheelbase (mm)	1500	1500	1500	1500
Seat height (mm)	800	800	800	800
Length (mm)	2250	2220	2220	2220
Width (mm)	700	700	700	700
Weight (kg)	210.5	195	212.5	196

Model	1000 MHR	750 F1	750 F1	750 Montjuich
Year	1984–85	1985	1986–87	1986
Bore (mm)	88	88	88	88
Stroke (mm)	80	61.5	61.5	61.5
Capacity (cc)	973	748	748	748
Compression ratio	9.3:1	9.3:1	9.3:1	9.3:1
Max rpm	7500	9000	9500	10,000
Valve timing inlet (open/close)	63° btdc 83° abdc	29° btdc 90° abdc	39° btdc 80° abdc	67° btdc 99° abdc
Valve timing exhaust (open/close)	80° bbdc 58° atdc	70° bbdc 48° atdc	80° bbdc 38° atdc	93° bbdc 70° atdc
Carburation	Dell'Orto PHM40B	Dell'Orto PHF36A	Dell'Orto PHF36A	Dell'Orto PHM40N
Front tyre	100/90V18	120/80V16	120/80V18	12/60-16
Rear tyre	130/90V18	130/80V18	130/80V18	18/67-16
Front brake (mm)	280 twin disc	280 twin disc	280 twin disc	280 twin disc
Rear brake (mm)	280 disc	260 disc	260 disc	260 disc
Wheelbase (mm)	1500	1400	1400	1400
Seat height (mm)	800	750	750	750
Length (mm)	2220	2110	2110	2110
Width (mm)	700	690	690	690
Weight (kg)	198	175	175	155

Model	750 Laguna Seca	750 Santa Monica	400 SS Jnr	900 SS
Year	1987	1988	1989–90	1989–90
Bore (mm)	88	88	70.5	92
Stroke (mm)	61.5	61.5	51	68
Capacity (cc)	748	748	398	904
Compression ratio	9.3:1	9.3:1	10:1	9.2:1
Max rpm	10,000	10,000	11,000	9000
Valve timing inlet (open/close)	67° btdc 99° abdc	67° btdc 99° abdc	31° btdc 88° abdc	20° btdc 60° abdc
Valve timing exhaust (open/close)	93° bbdc 70° atdc	93° bbdc 70° atdc	72° bbdc 46° atdc	58° bbdc 20° atdc
Carburation	Dell'Orto PHM40N	Dell'Orto PHM40N	Mikuni CVKV36	Webber 44 DCNF116
Front tyre	130/60ZR16	130/60VR16	130/60ZR16	130/60ZR17
Rear tyre	160/60ZR16	160/60VR16	160/60ZR16	130/60ZR17
Front brake (mm)	280 twin disc	280 twin disc	280 twin disc	300 twin disc
Rear brake (mm)	260 disc	260 disc	260 disc	245 disc
Wheelbase (mm)	1400	1400	1450	1450
Seat height (mm)	785	785	750	720
Length (mm)	2110	2110	2000	2040
Width (mm)	690	690	670	670
Weight (kg)	165	165	174	180

Model	350 S/SS	400 SS	750 SS	900 SS
Year	1991–93	1991–97	1991–93	1991–93
Bore (mm)	66	70.5	88	92
Stroke (mm)	51	51	61.5	68
Capacity (cc)	341	398	748	904
Compression ratio	10.7:1	10:1	9:1	9.2:1
Max rpm	11,000	11,000	9000	9000
Valve timing inlet (open/close)	31° btdc 88° abdc	31° btdc 88° abdc	31° btdc 88° abdc	20° btdc 60° abdc
Valve timing exhaust (open/close)	72° bbdc 46° atdc	72° bbdc 46° atdc	72° bbdc 46° atdc	58° bbdc 20° atdc
Carburation	Mikuni BDST38-B100	Mikuni BDST38-B79	Mikuni BDST38-B70	Mikuni BDST38-B67
Front tyre	120/60VR17	120/60VR17	120/60VR17	120/70ZR17
Rear tyre	160/60VR17	160/60VR17	160/60VR17	170/60ZR17
Front brake (mm)	320 disc	320 disc	320 disc	320 twin disc
Rear brake (mm)	245 disc	245 disc	245 disc	245 disc
Wheelbase (mm)	1410	1410	1410	1410
Seat height (mm)	770	770	780	780
Length (mm)	2000	2000	2020	2030
Width (mm)	730	730	710	730
Weight (kg)	169	173	173	183

Model	900 SL	900 SL	600 SS	750 SS
Year	1992	1993	1994–97	1994–97
Bore (mm)	92	92	80	88
Stroke (mm)	68	68	58	61.5
Capacity (cc)	904	904	583	748
Compression ratio	9.2:1	9.2:1	10.7:1	9:1
Max rpm	9000	9000	9000	9000
Valve timing inlet (open/close)	20° btdc 60° abdc	20° btdc 60° abdc	31° btdc 88° abdc	31° btdc 88° abdc
Valve timing exhaust (open/close)	58° bbdc 20° atdc	58° bbdc 20° atdc	72° bbdc 46° atdc	72° bbdc 46° atdc
Carburation	Mikuni BDST38-B67	Mikuni BDST38-B67	Mikuni BDST38-B156	Mikuni BDST38-B70
Front tyre	120/70VR17	120/70ZR17	120/60VR17	120/60VR17
Rear tyre	170/60VR17	170/60ZR17	160/60VR17	160/60VR17
Front brake (mm)	320 twin disc	320 twin disc	320 disc	320 twin disc
Rear brake (mm)	245 disc	245 disc	245 disc	245 disc
Wheelbase (mm)	1410	1410	1410	1410
Seat height (mm)	780	780	770	780
Length (mm)	2030	2030	2000	2020
Width (mm)	730	730	730	710
Weight (kg)	176	179	173	176

Model	900 CR	900 SL	900 SS	900 SS SP
Year	1994–98	1994–96	1994–96	1994–97
Bore (mm)	92	92	92	92
Stroke (mm)	68	68	68	68
Capacity (cc)	904	904	904	904
Compression ratio	9.2:1	9.2:1	9.2:1	9.2:1
Max rpm	9000	9000	9000	9000
Valve timing inlet (open/close)	43° btdc 85° abdc	20° btdc 60° abdc	43° btdc 85° abdc	43° btdc 85° abdc
Valve timing exhaust (open/close)	82° bbdc 46° atdc	58° bbdc 20° atdc	82° bbdc 46° atdc	82° bbdc 46° atdc
Carburation	Mikuni BDST38-B73	Mikuni BDST38-B67	Mikuni BDST38-B67	Mikuni BDST38-B73
Front tyre	120/70ZR17	120/70ZR17	120/70ZR17	120/70ZR17
Rear tyre	160/60ZR17	170/60ZR17	170/60ZR17	170/60ZR17
Front brake (mm)	320 twin disc	320 twin disc	320 twin disc	320 twin disc
Rear brake (mm)	245 disc	245 disc	245 disc	245 disc
Wheelbase (mm)	1410	1410	1410	1410
Seat height (mm)	780	750	780	780
Length (mm)	2000	2030	2000	2000
Width (mm)	730	730	730	730
Weight (kg)	186	182	186	186

Model	900 SS	900 SS FE	900 SS
Year	1997	1997–98	1998
Bore (mm)	92	92	92
Stroke (mm)	64	64	68
Capacity (cc)	904	904	904
Compression ratio	9.2:1	9.2:1	9.2:1
Max rpm	9000	9000	9000
Valve timing inlet (open/close)	24° btdc 70° abdc	24° btdc 70° abdc	25° btdc 75° abdc
Valve timing exhaust (open/close)	58° bbdc 29° atdc	58° bbdc 29° atdc	66° bbdc 28° atdc
Carburation	Mikuni BDST38-B67	Mikuni BDST38-B67	Marelli CPU 1.5 Injection
Front tyre	120/70ZR17	120/70ZR17	120/70ZR17
Rear tyre	170/60ZR17	170/60ZR17	170/60ZR17
Front brake (mm)	320 twin disc	320 twin disc	320 twin disc
Rear brake (mm)	245 disc	245 disc	245 disc
Wheelbase (mm)	1410	1410	1410
Seat height (mm)	780	780	800
Length (mm)	2030	2030	2030
Width (mm)	780	780	780
Weight (kg)	186	185	188

Production figures of Ducati Super Sport motorcycles, 1974–97

Model	350-400 SS	600 SS	750 Sport	750 SS	900 SS	900 SL	900 S2 kick	900 S2 electric	1000 S2	750 F1	350-400 F3	900 MHR	900 MHR electric	1000 MHR
Year														
1974	–	–	856	401	–	–	–	–	–	–	–	–	–	–
1975	–	–	–	249	246	–	–	–	–	–	–	–	–	–
1976	–	–	–	220	1020	–	–	–	–	–	–	–	–	–
1977	–	–	–	100	633	–	–	–	–	–	–	–	–	–
1978	–	–	23	30	1037	–	–	–	–	–	–	–	–	–
1979	–	–	–	–	1014	–	–	–	–	–	–	300	–	–
1980	–	–	–	–	833	–	–	–	–	–	–	447	–	–
1981	–	–	–	–	1205	–	–	–	–	–	–	1500	–	–
1982	–	–	–	–	335	–	173	476	–	–	–	1549	–	–
1983	–	–	–	–	–	–	180	202	–	–	–	780	687	–
1984	–	–	–	–	–	–	–	205	71	–	–	25	770	662
1985	–	–	–	–	–	–	–	–	100	628	–	–	–	200
1986	–	–	–	–	–	–	–	–	–	1377	976	–	–	250
1987	–	–	–	–	–	–	–	–	–	200	–	–	–	–
1988	–	–	1241	–	–	–	–	–	–	–	300	–	–	–
1989	300	–	1365	–	1471	–	–	–	–	–	–	–	–	–
1990	300	–	153	–	533	–	–	–	–	–	–	–	–	–
1991	500	–	–	1872	4305	–	–	–	–	–	–	–	–	–
1992	1051	–	–	1872	4305	1317	–	–	–	–	–	–	–	–
1993	950	–	–	2352	3853	861	–	–	–	–	–	–	–	–
1994	150	2355	–	1008	3365	719	–	–	–	–	–	–	–	–
1995	–	737	–	1550	4330	578	–	–	–	–	–	–	–	–
1996	200	463	–	60	1768	300	–	–	–	–	–	–	–	–
1997	200	801	–	1146	1594	500	–	–	–	–	–	–	–	–

Index

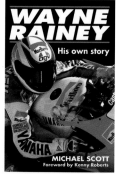
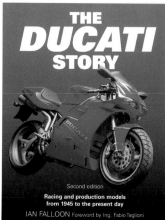
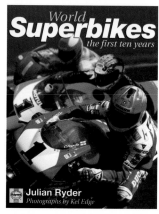
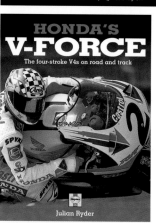
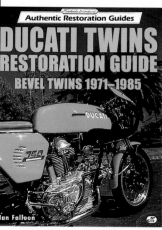
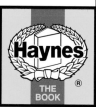